D1740022

THINK.
PLAN.
LIVE.

*Define and design your Best Life
in 6 simple steps*

GILL McLAREN

DEDICATION

To my amazing daughters, Ellen and Lucy
You constantly inspire and support me
This book is dedicated to you

First published in 2017 by Gill McLaren

© Gill McLaren 2017

The moral rights of the author have been asserted

All rights reserved. Except as permitted under the *Australian Copyright Act 1968* (for example, a fair dealing for the purposes of study, research, criticism or review), no part of this book may be reproduced, stored in a retrieval system, communicated or transmitted in any form or by any means without prior written permission.

All inquiries should be made to the author.

A catalogue entry for this book is available from the National Library of Australia.

ISBN: 978-1-925648-03-4

Printed in Australia by McPherson's Printing
Project management and text design by Michael Hanrahan Publishing
Cover design by Peter Reardon

Reprinted August 2017

The paper this book is printed on is certified as environmentally friendly.

Disclaimer

The material in this publication is of the nature of general comment only, and does not represent professional advice. It is not intended to provide specific guidance for particular circumstances and it should not be relied on as the basis for any decision to take action or not take action on any matter which it covers. Readers should obtain professional advice where appropriate, before making any such decision. To the maximum extent permitted by law, the author and publisher disclaim all responsibility and liability to any person, arising directly or indirectly from any person taking or not taking action based on the information in this publication.

Contents

Welcome to the world of *Think. Plan. Live.*

> 'What surprises me most is "Man", because he sacrifices his health in order to make money. Then he sacrifices money to recuperate his health. And then he is so anxious about the future that he doesn't enjoy the present; The result being he doesn't live in the present or the future; He lives as if he's never going to die, and then he dies having never really lived.'
>
> **Dalai Lama**

There is something powerfully reflective about getting roughly halfway through life and wondering to yourself, *Is this as good as it gets? Am I really living the life I want from a career and family perspective?* A remarkably high number of people have these thoughts – you've probably had them yourself. But then life gets busy again, and we park them. But those thoughts often pop back into our heads at regular intervals, and they never really go away.

You may think what I am referring to is a 'mid-life crisis'. Others may call it that, but I don't see it that way. I consider it more of a 'mid-life reflection'. This is the process of wondering more often and more deeply about whether you are making the most of your life. These thoughts are most commonly about career and family life, but you may also wonder if you are doing the best you can for the people you care about, such as your children, aging parents and close friends. For many people this pondering or reflection is often triggered by challenges you or your friends and family are going through, or by hearing about or seeing others go through difficulties. Although these situations may spark thoughts about what you are all about and how to make the best of life, most people let these thoughts come and go. Most people never address, once and for all, what these 'life' questions actually mean for them. The questions are often asked but rarely answered.

I felt the same way about life, until one day I received a big jolt to my thinking. I was sitting in the audience at a talk and one of the panellists in a discussion on work–life balance said, 'I don't believe in work–life balance and that it exists; I believe in living your best life. Living your best life is really working out what you want out of life, not what you think you should want or others say you should do but what you want. Once you work that out you will be so much happier with your life.'

YOUR BEST LIFE DESIGN

The concept of Best Life Design and discovering what that looks like for you and developing practical tools to get you there have been my personal focus for nearly a decade since that jolt I received listening to that panel. My journey and discoveries about how you design and live your best life had plenty of twists and turns: some things worked and some didn't. But I have now reached the point where I feel I can share my discoveries with others, which is why I wrote *Think. Plan. Live.* I want to help you and others navigate Life Design and provide all the practical tools needed to do this.

> 'The more that you read, the more things you will know. The more that you learn, the more places you'll go.'
>
> **Dr Seuss**

Think. Plan. Live. is a workbook designed to take you on a practical and pragmatic journey, complete with tried and tested strategic frameworks, tools and practical advice that will stimulate your own thinking so that you can confidently design a best life plan for yourself as unique to you as your fingerprint.

The chapters are laid out in a 6-step approach to define your **Who**, **What**, **With**, **Why**, **Where** and **When**, giving you all the stimulus, encouragement and practical tools you need to rediscover your strengths, values and passions, and to help you steer yourself back on track or to find a new path. After completing these steps, the book explores in more detail how you can integrate your learnings into your life, career and leadership style.

The methods and approaches are tried and tested by me over many years, as the culmination of my own history to date; in fact, I left a busy executive job to write this book! After a three-decade career in the corporate world it increasingly dawned on me that people are not as happy as they could be, driven largely by the fact that they feel stressed and overworked, and are juggling building a successful and rewarding career with devoting time to a great family and personal life. I experienced first-hand that unfortunately work pressures often take over and family balance goes out the window.

The opportunity became clear: owning the design of our best life would really help. Initially I started with myself, but I then came to realise my practical thinking and planning tools and approach worked for my colleagues, teams and friends too. Through coaching and mentoring hundreds of people, my thinking and my tools have evolved into what you see here.

Do you fundamentally believe that you shouldn't feel as though you have to choose between your career and your family, and that even though you don't know how, it should be possible to build a more purposeful life plan that enables you to achieve success in both aspects of life? If that's the case, that's all you need to get started. A natural curiosity to explore who you are and your life choices and an openness to apply some thinking and some feeling to how you show up in life – based on the experiences of others in the same shoes – are the keys to developing your own Best Life Design.

Although everyone likes the idea of living their best life (who wouldn't?), discovering practically how to achieve this is difficult and daunting at times, and without the right support it can feel like an unrealistic goal. I have written *Think. Plan. Live.* to be a practical 'buddy' to support you through the steps of designing and living your best life. To keep it practical I have included my own stories, real-life examples, tools and tips to help you think through for yourself what's important and to help you design and plan out your own best life. After all the time and effort you have put into life so far, I think you deserve to have a rewarding career and to enjoy time to spend with the family and friends you care about.

The goal is that by the end of the book you will feel inspired and positive about what Life Design could do for your career and personal life by you playing to your strengths, living up to your values, and leading with purpose in your career. Hopefully you picked up the book out of self-motivation to make a positive change for yourself and a desire to make a difference in the world. The book will give you an extra nudge and some practical tools to help you create and work through your plan.

NO TWO LIVES ON THE PLANET ARE THE SAME

> 'Let go of who you think you should be
> and embrace who you are.'
>
> **Brené Brown**

For Life Design to really, really work it has to be personalised and tailored 100% to *you*. There is way too much pressure out there to live up to the unrealistic expectations or judgements put upon us – often unwittingly – by others. A foundation principle of best life definition and design is that the only judge of whether you are living your best life or not is *you*, and *only* you. I came to the realisation through coaching and mentoring hundreds of people that no two lives on the planet are the same. We each have our own Life Fingerprint, and just as no two fingerprints are the same, your best life is completely unique to you. It is created from knowing who you are, what you love doing (that is, your purpose), and what people, places or careers bring out the best in you.

> 'There are those that look at things the way they are, and ask why? I dream of things that never were, and ask why not?'
>
> **Robert F. Kennedy**

The goal of this book is to re-stimulate your own ambition to make the best out of life and to make a difference. The book has loads of practical exercises, scientific frameworks and research, plus real stories and tips, and they all have one aim, and one aim only: to enable you to think about your own Sparks and Jolts in life that got you to where you are now and to help you gather those thoughts into a practical, forward-looking best life plan for yourself.

The book is modular and easy to navigate, and focuses on experiences and practical tools that are proven to be the successful building blocks of Life Design. *Think. Plan. Live.* aims to help you get to know yourself, to find your sources of inspiration, to find ways to unlock time, to define and build the right next career and leadership step, and to build a rewarding personal life with your family and friends.

STRATEGIC PLANNING FOR LIFE

> 'Always be a first rate version of yourself and not a second rate version of someone else.'
>
> **Judy Garland**

I am now able to look back on my journey so far and feel pride that I navigated a successful executive career in the business world while working across three continents. I did so while being a mum to now teenage twin daughters, and being a compassionate and authentic leader in my own style. My journey to create this approach to best life planning was a thread running through my nearly 30-year career working for big corporates, the last 20 years of which was with one of the biggest international companies: Coca-Cola.

The turning point for me was realising that the strategic planning and business planning approaches I used to build strategic business plans could be equally applied to Life Design planning. When I shared this philosophy and approach with others, they too started to practise parts of it. I suddenly came to a realisation that what I had come to take for granted as my way of planning out my life, others regarded as a new approach that really helped them. That created a massive Jolt in me. I realised that sharing this approach was what needed to be done, and *Think. Plan. Live.* was created.

What I found was that, although people find the idea of designing a rewarding career and great personal life exciting, they also feel it's daunting and unattainable. If it was that easy, everyone would do it ... right? That's true. The problems generally stem from people deciding that they should define their best life in comparison to the lives of others. But the danger of comparing ourselves to others is that it creates unrealistic expectations; *they have a better job, a more supportive family, a nicer house or car, they are smarter and luckier than me.* The list goes on and on, and people end up with an unrealistic idea of what they should be aiming for in life. This is an even bigger problem today in the social media age. If you contrast that with the goal of defining *your* best life that is as unique to you as your fingerprint, the need for comparison goes away. Your goal becomes to make your life the best it can be for you and those you care about.

Reading and using the tools in *Think. Plan. Live.* will help you reconnect with what is important to you and discover what your unique talents and gifts are, and then convert these discoveries into a career, authentic leadership and a best life that 'fits' *you*.

> 'Everybody is a genius. But if you judge a fish by its ability to climb a tree, it will live its whole life believing that it is stupid.'
>
> **Albert Einstein**

The approach I have developed to help you discover your Life Fingerprint is, by its nature, very different to the approaches to development I have encountered during my career. Most of the tools for personal development are assessment tools which are designed to ... well ... assess you (or put another way, judge you ...), to classify you or put you in a box. My realisation – after going through my career and experiencing and being developed by this training – is that none of them started with a discovery of 'me' or really helped me to amplify me ... and to be truly myself. My goal is you will experience the tools developed for the Life Fingerprint as discovery rather than assessment tools. It's all about amplifying who you are.

My hope is that *Think. Plan. Live.* will be a practical guide to people who want to build a life more in tune with their purpose and who have a desire to make a difference.

So let's get started with planning your best life.

Gill McLaren

Chapter 1

How to create a strategic plan for your Life

> 'The most difficult thing is the decision to act, the rest is merely tenacity. The fears are paper tigers. You can do anything you decide to do; you can act to change and control your life.'
>
> **Amelia Earhart**

I felt 'Life Design' was the best way to describe my approach to mapping out your 'best life' because it is a fully owned design job from start to finish. During the design journey you must make some choices and trade-offs in different areas and in what you want the finished project to look like. First you make the plan, then you set about achieving it.

Where do you start when designing your best life? Before you can make any plans – in life or in business – you must first develop an accurate picture of where you are now. So, let's get into it!

YOUR LIFE PLAN: THE MOST IMPORTANT PLAN YOU'LL EVER WRITE

Over my corporate career I created many business plans. As part of this process I looked at a SWOT analysis (**S**trengths, **W**eaknesses, **O**pportunities and **T**hreats) to:

- assess what we were currently doing well and what we were doing poorly
- define opportunity areas in line with our strengths and capabilities
- help set a vision and targets to define and achieve our goals.

Based on this analysis I then mobilised a plan to get us to our destination, constantly honing and adapting the plan and the execution of it to get results. Business and strategic planning is proven – it works! If you are in business you will be more than familiar with this approach, and may also have many business plans under your belt. If not, the approach will hopefully sound intuitive to you. (And don't worry – business expertise is not a prerequisite for focusing on and planning your life … everyone can do Life Design, no matter what their skills and experience.)

When I thought about my life and quizzed myself on whether I planned it with the same rigour as the business and strategic plans I was so adept at creating, of course the answer was *no*. So, I set about remedying that. How would I do it? What tools or frameworks would help? Where could I source inspiration from?

I was a work in progress for a while (still am …), but after developing and adapting how I felt and thought about my life, I came up with an approach that really worked. But, even though I knew it really worked for me, I didn't initially see it could work for others too. But as I started to share my approach with other people, it really sparked interest, and this got me thinking how great it would be if I could walk people through the approach in a book. So that's what I've sought to do, making *Think. Plan. Live.* a workbook to your journey of building a strategic plan for yourself. After all, writing a best life plan for you has to be more important than any other plan you write. No-one wants to feel life is passing them by, or be left wondering *is this as good as it gets?*

You are the architect and the builder

Before committing the approach to paper in this book, I have tried and tested the tools and frameworks on myself, plus a spectrum of other people, including senior executive coaching clients, start-up founders, workshop attendees and friends, so I can now hand on heart say and know it definitively works. The core premise of Life Design is, the only person who can design your future life is *you*. You are the architect and the builder.

Now I often hear people at this point saying things like:

- 'I don't feel in control, and I'm no architect.'

- 'So much stuff is happening – I am just trying to get through it.'

- 'I'm juggling too many things.'

- 'I've no time to think.'

- 'My life is not about me because of everyone else I need to care for.'

- 'My work is what it is – it's all consuming and I just need to get on with it.'

And on and on it goes. These statements about life are true for most people, but that doesn't mean they *have* to be your reality. You can of course continue to live day to day, trying to work through each challenge piecemeal as best you can. And in reality, that's what most people do. But what I've found is that with a bit of thinking and reflection about your life and what's important – and, even more critically, what's not – we can reconnect with what really matters and design and shape our life path to be more about what we want and need.

What I have found is that often the most effective adjustments we can make are tweaks and small shifts that together create a massive difference. There is usually no need to completely re-plan your life – in design terms it's a renovation rather than a knock down and rebuild. In most cases it's about being honest with ourselves. When being honest, most people know where their problems lie, but just defining them and being aware of them does not create change. It takes being clear on what you'd rather life be like to create a mindset shift, and once that has happened anything is possible.

In many cases we have let some things drop off the radar that are important to us, and we may just need to reconnect with and find time for them.

Some examples from my coaching clients are:

- spending a bit more time with close friends
- travelling more
- picking up that hobby again
- having more 'me' time
- finding time for work de-stressors, such as exercise or time with the kids.

Making life happen

Shifting to *Life Design* instead of *life reactions* means you get back in control and stay in the driver's seat. It just takes a simple but critically important reframe, from *life happens to me* to *I make life happen*.

The goal is not some perfect Life Design that means you don't have to react any more; of course life will still throw stuff at you all the time. But what I can confidently say is that if you have thought about where you are trying to head and what your life priorities are, you can react positively when problems arise and proactively recognise opportunities in a way that reflects your goals in life. As the old adage goes, 'When life gives you lemons, make lemonade'. Or another option I like even more: 'When life gives you lemons, make gin and tonic'.

If you think about your best life you can shape your existence more into what you want it to be, and so become more resilient when facing the inevitable curve balls and difficulties along the way.

Sparks and Jolts

As you read this book and complete the exercises, read the stories and try out the frameworks, it is your thoughts that count. Some parts will resonate or connect more than others – that's okay. What connects the most for you will be dependent on what's going on for you at work or in your broader life. Pay particular attention to what you are thinking and feeling as you read through the book, and if what you read triggers something take a minute to think about it versus letting it be a passing thought (trust me – these thoughts and feelings pop into your head for a reason …). Some of these will be 'a-ha' moments or 'Sparks' in you, and for other moments the feeling will be much greater – these are our 'Jolts'.

Please read on with the mindset that you are going to really think about what the content means to you. I wrote this book to be a collection of stimuli, to share some of what works for me and other people I have helped. But, given your unique Life Fingerprint, what resonates with you is unique to you and is all about you …

Synthesis, Synergy and Integration

My Life Design process is an iterative one, and it seeks to uncover who we are and what we really want, versus who we are being or think we should be. My method to create Life Design is in three phases:

- **Synthesis:** is to first look at all the information from your life to date and create a Synthesis of this into patterns of recurring behaviours, attitudes, values, strengths, life highs and life lows.

- **Synergy:** is about finding patterns in who we are and in life themes on what drives, inspires and energises us, and in what we attach greatest priority and importance to.

- **Integration:** is when it all comes together into a final plan for you. What aspects of your life are you happy with and which aspects would you like to optimise and develop? The Integration plans start with simple, easy-to-do next steps, but also for many people this will define future goal setting, career shifts and retirement planning.

So, given the journey of Life Design is about joining the dots, and capturing all the inputs to these dots, and building them into an integrated life plan, it is important you capture your thoughts, Sparks and Jolts as you experience them. While you are on the journey of Life Design this book will act as a good stimulus, but what it also does is sensitise you to observe how you are living your life each minute. As I will cover more in the next chapter in my story of how I became a 'self-anthropologist', I became much more in tune with my own behaviours during this process, and also where my triggers, motivations, energy sources and inspirations came from. I would encourage you to become a self-anthropologist too! If that concept sounds a bit strange to start with, don't worry – that's normal! Just start with the Synthesis part, which is all about paying more attention to your own behaviours and writing down your thoughts as you go.

LIFE DESIGN

Synthesis	Chapter 2: <u>Who</u>	
Define who you are and what matters to you	• My Life Line • My Values • My Strengths	**Who**
Synergy *Develop your compass and define your work and personal priorities*	Chapter 3: <u>What</u> • My Sources of Inspiration • My Life Wheel	**What**
	Chapter 4: <u>With</u> • My Energy Sources	**With**
	Chapter 5: <u>Why</u> • My Gifts and my Why	**Why**
Integration *Build 12-month and milestone forward life plans*	Chapter 6: <u>Where</u>	**Where**
	Chapter 7: <u>When</u> • Autobiography and Biography • Life Plan 12 months • Life Plan Milestones	**When**

I have created the book to also be your notepad to collect your thoughts. Use the pages provided to jot down your thoughts as they come to the fore. The notes pages at the back of the book plus in each chapter can be used to capture your Sparks and Jolts as you go. When you have one of these feelings, simply write down what the Spark or Jolt was and how it made you feel, and if you have any initial thoughts on what you want to do about it. Just get in the habit of writing them down – no need to overthink them – as you go through the book. Some Sparks and Jolts will build as you make progress, so keep adding to them. Don't overthink what they mean, just capture the thoughts and feelings that pop up, as they happen.

> 'Live as if you were to die tomorrow.
> Learn as if you were to live forever.'
>
> **Mahatma Gandhi**

HOW TO SPOT A JOLT MOMENT

Why have I become so passionate about Life Design? One goal sits behind this for me: to fully live the 'best life' I can before I die. This may seem a morbid thought, but interestingly, contemplating death can have a remarkable impact on life – it certainly did for me. Here's a bit more context on my personal Jolts ... I've learned with clients I have coached – and in myself too – that some of the biggest Jolts and Sparks have come at the low points of their lives. To start with I thought it was just me, but what I have realised from my coaching work in Best Life Design is that both our highs and lows define us, but particularly our lows. There is something about when you fail that causes you to learn and think about what happened, but when you succeed you usually cruise on and don't learn. There is something we draw on in a low that stops us in our tracks and makes us think; our resilience kicks in and changes what happens after that moment.

I have realised for me, as for many others, major turning points can be caused by a reaction to feelings of sadness or regret. There is something about those emotions that I find drives me towards much deeper self-reflection, and through that I get into much deeper self-insights on 'what I am doing in my life?'

One such Jolt that completely changed my life, and was the impetus for leaving a successful corporate career to pursue Life Design, was paying attention to the impact the experience of losing two inspiring colleagues had on me, and my story with each of them.

The Coca-Cola Asia Pacific leadership teams would gather annually for major strategic meetings. I got to meet some amazing colleagues and learn about the different cultures and their markets and the challenges they faced. The meetings rotated around different countries, and as well as the hard work we put into those sessions we also had plenty of time for fun and socialising along the way. Through these meetings I met Shelley, who led the marketing team in Japan. She was an amazing lady; smart, practical, a great marketer and a great leader, plus also energetic and full of fun. She was one of those people I just clicked with. We didn't work together that much, but at those Asia Pacific meetings we always caught up for a chat, mostly socially to share stories and a laugh. She had a great sense of humour and a very quick wit.

In 2014 she was on an overseas business trip as part of a group from different countries from around the world. The group gathered in the hotel lobby getting ready to head out for the day. Shelley was there chatting to people, and then realised she had left something in her hotel room, so she headed to the lifts and back to her room. She never returned to that lobby. After several minutes people went to check on her. Tragically, she was found in her room having suffered a major heart attack. An amazing woman had left us at the age of 40.

News of the tragic loss shocked all who knew Shelley, and everyone was united in sadness. They were also united in recognition and reflection of what an amazing person she was. People shared stories and made videos to mourn her loss but also to celebrate her life and what she brought to the world. My thoughts went out to her family and close friends and colleagues. It hit me hard too, in a way that took me aback a little, and the tragedy made me really start to think and reflect about my life in a way that started to scare me. This was definitely a Jolt. If I were to die, what legacy would I leave in the world? Would I have lived up to my potential? Would I have made a difference? What would people say about me?

This reflection gave me some comfort in the sense that I knew I was cared about and that people would miss me and say nice things about me, but in terms of my legacy and all the things I wanted to achieve in life I still felt there was a big gap and I needed more answers. My reflections intensified ... I thought deeply about my life, my leadership, how good a mum I was, and how I was showing up. Despite the unease that I perhaps wasn't living my best life, I reassured myself that life was still pretty good and everything was 'fine', so I parked these thoughts. I got practical and threw myself back into work.

That was until I was Jolted once more on hearing the news in the same year of a dear colleague back in the UK called Robert, who had been diagnosed with Hodgkin lymphoma. Early treatments seemed to go well, so the signs were good. But then I heard the news that he had taken a step back, and they realised that a stem cell or bone marrow donor was needed. However, his tissue type was incredibly rare, and no match could be found. Across the company, I and so many other people Robert had connected with signed up as potential donors. All that was needed was a swab of cells from your cheek and you could be assessed for a match. The procedure to donate marrow would be a painful one, but everyone willingly signed up in the hope that somehow we would be the rare match he was looking for.

The other inspiring part of this was that Robert's three daughters mobilised a campaign via social media to increase donors. They appeared in a number of national newspapers and on television, and their Facebook page generated 47,000 likes. The related donor charity received a surge in people testing to be a match.

Through the illness it was amazing to see the strength of feeling and support that family, friends and colleagues provided for Robert. Plus, Robert himself chronicled his own journey and reflections in updates and articles.

I had known Robert the whole of my 20-year Coca-Cola career. Although he was much more senior to me when I joined, we had connected from the start, drawn together by a shared irreverent English sense of humour (which I have realised is a theme in my life!), and also a real belief in how to build relationships with customers and to build collaborative teams. Robert was my mentor and ultimately my sponsor to secure my first customer general management role, but what set him apart was that he was an amazing leader who gave his time selflessly to others, no matter how junior they were. He also gave me one of the most pivotal pieces of coaching I ever received when I was embarking on my first major leadership role:

> Gill, you have reached the point in your career where it's not about you anymore; you may be great at what you do, that's

why I gave you the role, but from here on in it's not about you, it's all about how well you can inspire and motivate your team to deliver great things.

His advice really resonated with me, and I have sought to take that approach ever since.

Even after I left the UK we stayed in touch. We connected at major meetings, and while I was living and working in Malaysia he visited and we reconnected with laughs and stories like we had always done.

Robert's rare donor needs meant that despite the heroic efforts of his wife, daughters and others, none of the thousands of samples were a match, and he tragically passed away in September 2015, aged 58. Dauntingly for me he was only 10 years older than I was. This didn't feel like much time, and again I returned to thoughts of what my next decade should look like.

The tragedy of another loss gave me another unexpected Jolt. I reflected that although I had for some time been planning my best life, and at some point in the future my life had a chapter in it where I set up a business to focus on this, there was no urgency because I was also happy in my career. On the face of it life was good, but in my mind I knew that I had developed an approach to life that could really help people, and I was selfishly sitting on that … it was my wake-up call to make a life change, and to write *Think. Plan. Live.*

It took tragedy to help me see that in myself, and what I have since realised from coaching people is that life's highs and lows, personal tragedies and triumphs, terrible and great bosses, and positive and bad experiences are often triggers, but not always triggers we pay sufficient attention to. Interestingly, what I also found is that the lows create much stronger reactions than the highs, because they force us to draw on our resilience to fix a situation or make it better. (Completing the Life Line exercise in the next chapter you may notice the same. So when you get to it, give it some time and thought.) My hope is that by proactively mapping your Life Fingerprint and acting on its insight on you, it won't take a tragedy for you to create the change you want to see in your life. Not that I am proposing a corporate quit, or suggesting you relive my story – far from it. My proposal is that you write the current and future narrative for your own life.

A life without regrets

So why am I sharing my story? Not because my losses were unique; others have suffered similarly, and also in much greater ways. And it's not to say that the answer is to make the dramatic move of leaving a successful career to follow a different path; that was my answer to find my calling, but is certainly not for everyone. The reason I've shared these stories is we all have moments, events and circumstances that trigger deeper thoughts and reflections and deeper latent emotions centred around what life is all about. That is universal. However, what is not universal is what you do with such thoughts. Do you brush them off and move on, or really pause and think about your thoughts and feelings? If we all take that simple extra step of paying attention to what we are feeling in both the highs and lows of our lives, we will find in those situations the clues about what we really want out of life. The sobering thought out of this is it is better to use those thoughts to channel positive change in our lives than wait to the end and look back with regrets.

I live with the aim of having no regrets at the end of my life about what I should or could have done differently. Instead, I will practically work through my thoughts and feelings along the way, and handle them the best I can, so I know I'm being me and living the best life I am capable of. That is *my* best life, not anyone else's glossy version of an ideal life – pure and simple.

Why is this important? It's important because of the scary fact that studies consistently show that as people come to the end of their lives they start feeling sadness and regret for what they didn't do, achieve, share with others, or say. If your goal is that you don't want to have any of these regrets yourself, start living your best life now. Don't wait.

Apply your own oxygen mask first

Remember, *starting with you* is a bit like applying the safety advice on planes: 'If there is a drop in cabin pressure, oxygen masks will appear. Put on your own mask before assisting others.'

At the Integration phase of life planning, mapping your life with others you care about is a significant and important part of the journey. The reason I don't start there is that I find many people are so selfless that they make sure everyone else is okay first and don't pay enough attention to themselves and what really matters. I find people become lost in the fog of what they think they 'should' do or feel is expected of them versus what they really want.

WHO DO YOU THINK YOU ARE?

Have you ever seen the television program *Who Do You Think You Are?* It helps celebrities trace back into their ancestry and discover their family tree, finding relatives and stories they never knew about, and in many cases taking them on journeys all over the world to trace their heritage. I love watching the program because it's history brought to life, but I particularly enjoy seeing the transformation people feel learning more about their history, because it triggers them to think about themselves and creates a connection with 'who they think they are'.

> 'Today you are You, that is truer than true.
> There is no one alive who is Youer than You.'
>
> **Dr Seuss**

The more I explored, thought about and worked with the idea of Best Life Design, the more it struck me that what is special is the uniqueness of who we are and the lives we lead. *No-one* will travel the same life journey as you, or will have the same hopes, dreams and experiences, so we should all throw comparisons to others out the window and start with a deeper look at the main project; that is, ourselves. To devise a best life, funnily enough we need to know what one looks like for *us* – not for other people but for ourselves. In the same way that no two fingerprints are the same, no two lives are the same. Each life has a unique fingerprint to it, and at the heart of Best Life Design is working out what that Life Fingerprint is.

Your Life Fingerprint

Let's rewind back to the beginning of time ... well, *your* time. The day you were born: Day 1. You were born into the world with a certain pre-set conditioning: your DNA from your parents, your surrounding family, the environment you were in, your IQ. On Day 1 of your journey on the planet, you were dealt a set of playing cards that shaped you. From Day 1 the clock started ticking, and how you played the 'game called life' was shaped by your environment, surroundings, parental influence, school, university, friends, relationships, travel, work, health … the list of life stimuli goes on and on. New stimuli and inputs to who we are and who we become happen to us from Day 1 to the present day, whatever age you are now. The genes and IQ you were born with plus the external environment and influences you were surrounded by shaped you to be who you are, and your life to date has all been an input to how you show up in the world today. That nearly 50 years of input in my case was where I looked for clues to define and shape what my best life looked like.

What I have discovered is that our Life Fingerprint is well and truly defined by the time we reach adult life. Certain patterns of behaviour will recur, our highs and lows have triggers that have themes and patterns, and our values and strengths are well established too. But even though these patterns are set and are part of who you are, and your Life Fingerprint has already been defined by them, just because it's there doesn't mean it's visible to you. Up to 70,000 thoughts whiz through your head each day, usually with only the occasional thought devoted to yourself, so pondering what pattern your life is following clearly doesn't get much time.

If you could visualise your life as a fingerprint, what would be the patterns and grooves and shapes of thinking that would define it? That question is core to Best Life Design: define your Life Fingerprint and you have laid the foundations of Life Design. Easy to say, but hard to do … and this is the core theme of this book. How do I deeply *think* about it, *plan* for it, and ultimately *live* my life true to who I really am as defined by my Life Fingerprint? From the Jolt I received to define and live my best life nearly a decade ago, I have been on a journey to build a methodology and approach that would systematically help me and ultimately others bring to the surface what our Life Fingerprint looks like. This theme will be a recurring theme throughout this book, and in the subsequent chapters you will find exercises and tools that will help you take steps to bring you great clarity on your Life Fingerprint. Once that's clear, Best Life Design will come into sharper focus too.

So if your Life Fingerprint is already developed, your choice is whether you seek to discover it or leave it hidden and unexplored. Either way, have no doubt that it still exists and shows up in your attitudes and behaviours and in your strengths, your values and your passions. Think of the discovery of your Life Fingerprint like an iceberg – parts of your

Life Fingerprint are visible on the surface, other areas you may not have focused on or paid attention to even though you know they are important to you.

THE 6WS: WHO, WHAT, WITH, WHY, WHERE, WHEN

Best Life Design seeks to help you discover all elements of the Fingerprint using a 6Ws framework. The 6Ws are:

- Who
- What
- With
- Why
- Where
- When.

Let's have a look at each of these.

Who

Who captures the core of who you are – your strengths, your values and what drives your highs and lows, bringing out the best and worst in you. When you read your summary of your **Who** it will feel right and like a true summary. It sounds obvious to do this, to guide particularly work and career choices, but in most cases practicality has kicked in at some point in life and who you are got lost ... The exercises coming up of Life Line, Values and Strengths are the component parts of defining your 'Who ... am I?'

What

What focuses on what you enjoy doing – the type of work and career you enjoy and thrive in, and the hobbies, experiences and interests you enjoy. Once you have clarified what you enjoy doing, you can consider how what you currently do compares with that.

With

With puts the lens on who you enjoy doing things with – your family and friends, and also the colleagues or bosses that bring out the best in you too. It focuses on who and what gives you energy and inspiration and who and what takes these away. People either bring out the best or worst in us. We have more say and more opportunity than we think to control who we choose to spend time with. It's an active choice. It's at the core of actively managing our energy and inspiration levels. Because as humans we have a base need to fit in and belong, getting the **With** part of the Life Design puzzle wrong has in my experience the biggest impact on levels of self-confidence, self-esteem and happiness.

Why

My definition of your **Why** seeks to look beyond the area of purpose ... asking yourself why you do what you do is a good place to start. **Why** determines – based on your **Who**, **What**, **With** and your unique blend of strengths, values, belief and passions – what your 'gifts' are, the things that are uniquely you, that when you show up using this blend of what you do with who you are, you are at your absolute best, feeling energised and passionate. I have come to realise that people struggle to define their own 'gifts'; they are hidden from them because they are by their nature intuitive and come naturally. If this is the case, we often dismiss them as being normal and think everyone does things that way. They are in fact the opposite – unique and our greatest asset. We will explore more on how to capture your gifts in chapter 5.

Where

Where is all about places and environments that bring out the best in you. This is an area that doesn't generally get too much thought, but if you think about it, most people can identify the best environments for them. Countryside or city? Travelling or at home? On the beach or in a forest? What's your ideal home, your ideal work environment? With a bit of thought (and feeling), we all could visualise these places and pay attention to the physical spaces where we feel at our best and worst.

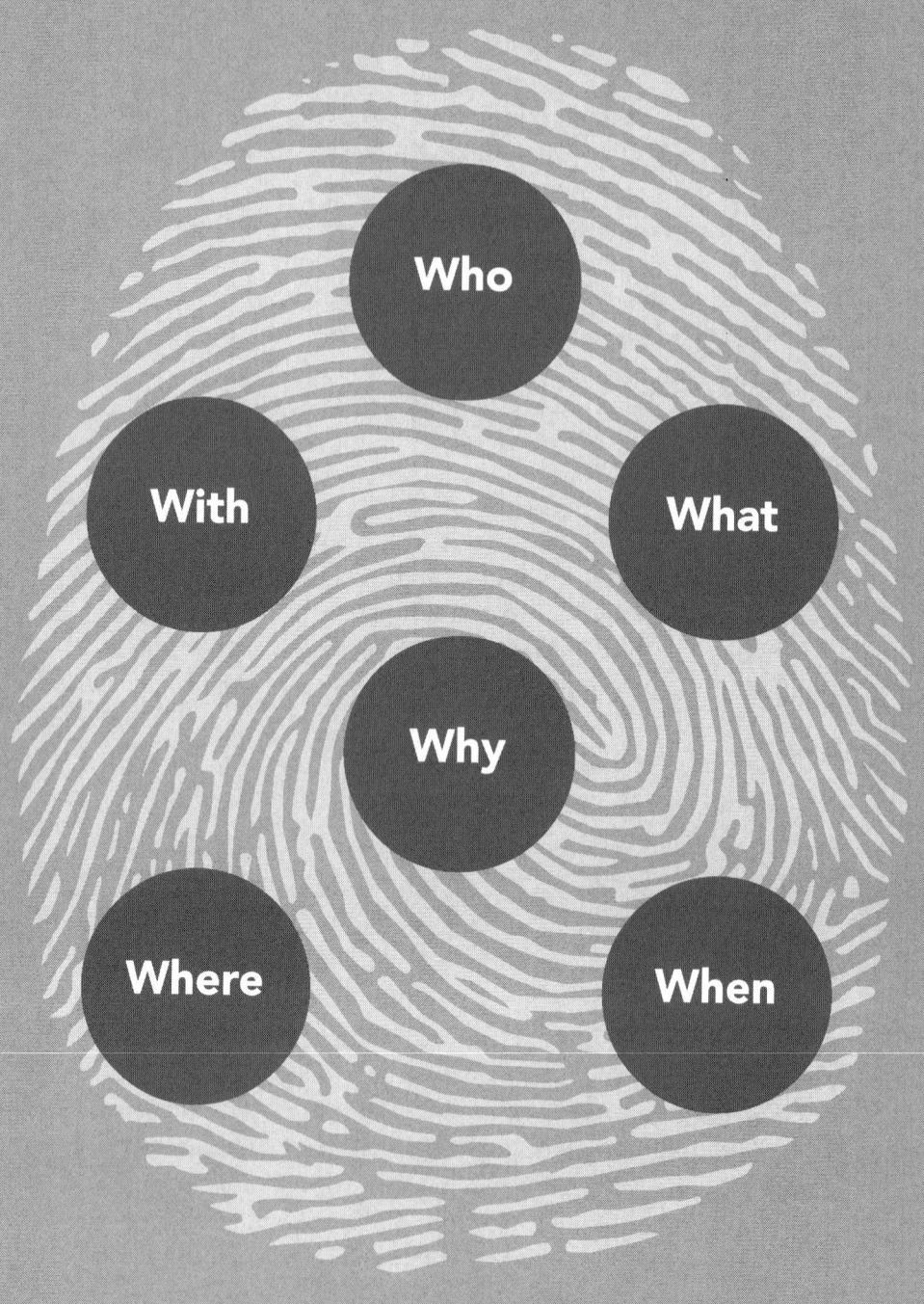

When

When is the final part of Life Design. It focuses when you want to do and achieve things against key milestones you determine. What would success look like in the next 12 months? When do I want to shift roles or careers? When do I want to start my own business? When do I want to move overseas or live back in my home country? When do I want to retire? Creating integrated plans against key personal milestones becomes intuitive, but only once the other 5Ws are clear.

* * *

Reading about these 6Ws may have intuitively triggered some Sparks for you on the answers to each of them, but for many people I coach and run workshops with, although there is a desire to know their answers to the 6Ws, thinking them through and reflecting on them so they 'feel right' is a blend of art and science. This is where the tools and frameworks I have created and included in the book come in. Many of these approaches are simple in construct; some are my own, some are my versions of classic coaching tools, some are neuroscience learnings. What I have sought to do is blend them together in sequence to take you on a journey so you become fully aware of who you really are (which is not always how you are showing up currently!), building that into an integrated life plan. The end result is a Life Design and Fingerprint purposefully designed by you, rather than one shaped by situation, circumstances and a career that wasn't congruent with what it ideally should have been.

I applied the 6Ws to Life Design and they form the component parts of the Life Fingerprint, not to help you delve back into your ancestry (albeit I do recommend that too at some point in your life!) but to build and capture, in a simple summary, a deeper understanding of who you really are as a person. Reflections about yourself through the 6Ws are the building blocks of life design.

Anyone from a business, commercial or research background may have come across a version of the 6Ws before. There are many applications for this methodology. I have previously applied the 6Ws in the context of strategic planning and research. To understand the motivations of consumer purchase decisions at Coca-Cola, we applied the 6Ws as the primary strategic tool to map the consumer beverage landscape in every country in the world. We captured all the drinks people consumed (including tap water, hot drinks, cold drinks – *every* drink), looking at **Who** was drinking, **What** they were drinking, **Why** they chose to drink, what they drank **With** (such as with food or by itself), **When** they drank, and **Why** they drank (thirst, for energy, to be social). These insights were the bedrock of the strategic choices we made on how to develop, segment and innovate in beverages.

Think. Plan. Live. is designed to support you to design and build your best life via the creation of your Life Fingerprint over the course of reading the book. Each chapter ends with a component part of your fingerprint and is captured in the summary at the end of each of the 6Ws chapters.

DEFINING YOUR OWN LIFE FINGERPRINT

So what makes up *you*? It's funny how little time most of us really spend on ourselves, thinking about who we are and what we want from life.

Thinking about what you want to achieve from life – and I mean *really* pausing and thinking – is the oxygen you need before you can do anything else.

Exploring what makes you ... well, you

We really do need to start with ourselves before we can, as we do in later chapters, devote time to thinking about who we are building that life with. Most people feel at times an overwhelming need to make sure they are doing the right thing by others. Am I creating the right environment and opportunities for my children to be happy and become great human beings? Is my work great? Does my boss value what I do? Are my aging parents alright – they seemed a bit down at the weekend? Is my marriage alright, with enough time for just the two of us? Thoughts like these and many more whiz through our heads at an alarming rate of knots.

After processing all of these thoughts, most people's self-diagnosis on 'How is my life?' is *it's okay, it's fine, it's good enough*, or the most common *it's pretty full on now, but it will calm down and get better later*. This conclusion of 'I'll tackle it later' is a very dangerous one. 'Later' typically means parking that thought in another part of our brain. The hamster wheel of life continues, and we think we will get to the big, important stuff eventually. I hate to disappoint you but later rarely arrives; if you really want to plan and work things out it takes some deep 'me' thinking time about who you are to find patterns and meaning in those thousands upon thousands of thoughts.

The other interesting part is, despite having all these thoughts, less than 5% of our daily thoughts are actually about ourselves. In fact, we are lucky if we give such weighty questions even a passing thought. Test yourself on this: when was the last time you asked yourself one of these questions:

- What are my hopes and dreams in life?

- What do I value?

- What am I good at?

- What is keeping me in a job where I don't feel I am fully valued?

- What do I love doing?

We usually devote very little time to ourselves and with ourselves to really work things out. 'With yourself' means really thinking about these questions for **Who** you are. These are all 'I' thoughts. Once your 'me' or 'I' thoughts are clear they can be followed by thoughts on **What, With, Why, When** and **Where**.

> 'The two most important days in your life are the day you are born and the day you find out why.'
>
> **Mark Twain**

This approach I have personally lived by, and I can honestly say hand on heart it worked and continues to work for me. The simple statement of 'live your best life', which I heard while listening to a panel discussion a decade ago, was a massive Jolt for me. I was doing great at work, I was a senior director at Coca-Cola, I was surrounded by colleagues I really enjoyed working with, I had a happy marriage, two amazing twin daughters and a great group of friends – what more could I hope for? But the honest answer to the question of whether it was my *best* life was far from an emphatic *yes*. It was a good life, a rewarding life, but also a full-on 24/7 life with all work and life boundaries blurred. I was feeling under pressure and worn out, and I was not feeling like I was reaching my full life potential. The other more morbid thought that crept into my head was if I died at that minute, I would not have left the legacy I wanted to leave.

So, that simple idea of living my best life quite frankly changed my life from that point on – it hit me at my core. It was a massive Jolt. 'Living my best life' became the mantra that I have lived by ever since. Without being melodramatic (which I'm not in life …), this piece of simple wisdom changed my life.

I'm a big thinker (it's no coincidence that the word *think* is in the title of this book …), so I spent a long time – in fact, the next decade of my life – thinking about what a 'best life' is. My most insightful 'thinking' times seem to be when I'm asleep – I will suddenly wake up at 4 am with some blinding insight. The other time I think really well is on long-haul flights when I am travelling alone, with far too much time on my hands, so I think …

My reflection on the concept of a best life is that far too often we strive for perfection, and that what we think a best life looks like is often based on observing the lives of those around us. This comparative approach to living is typically debilitating and demotivating, because somebody else's life, their possessions and their aspirations are guaranteed to be different to our own, and very often we can easily see other people's successes but not their struggles.

Although we are born with aspects of our life defined, such as our base IQ or our level of extraversion or introversion, much of our Fingerprint is developed over our life journey. In this regard we are responsible for our own evolution, our own development. We can manage and curate vital elements such as our sources of energy and our sources of inspiration.

With a little bit of thinking, reflection and planning you can unlock how you really feel about your life, and once you have done that you will never look back. If I reflect on how I came to work out what the barriers and drivers of building a great life are, it boils down to a few things. How we define ourselves is at the core of it. In your brain is an embedded story of who you are and what defines you; think of it as your life soundtrack. It is the collection of events from your childhood to the present day, and the people, experiences, major events and relationships that shaped you. When you were born, Day 1 of 'Project You' began. At that point, you were already the result of your parents' genes, and Life Design had begun. 'Project You' is exactly that: a project, a constant work in progress, that builds over the course of your life. Always building, always growing, always evolving. We are each a unique project of human evolution!

As you know, arriving in the world was just the start – most science now recognises that who we are in the world is a blend of nature and nurture. IQ has already been defined on Day 1; nature has dealt us a hand on what our intellect level is. Emotional Intelligence (EQ), on the other hand, seems to be a real blend of nature and nurture. How we emotionally respond to the world, our values and how we define ourselves are heavily defined first by our parents or who looks after us in the early years, and subsequently by relationship events with other people we meet along our path. Human interaction is an amazing thing. The behaviour that results as an output of our relationships with others forms the biggest part of who we are and how we show up in the world.

Our life is shaped by our experiences. Living means we are exposed to the elements, and just like a landscape is shaped and sculpted by wind, rain, water and temperature, we are shaped by people, experiences, learning, relationships, pain and pleasure. Our Life Fingerprint is crafted and contoured by these experiences ... that is what makes each of us unique.

NEUROSCIENCE AND WHAT IT MEANS FOR LIFE DESIGN

As well as the exercises I've included in the book aimed at helping you reflect, I also wanted to include a snapshot on the neuroscience that confirmed for me that my approach had validity beyond my own 30 years of work experience and life anthropology. Life Design by its nature is both art and science: the art of working out what's important to us and then living by it has a great deal of science behind explaining why we are as we are, and our behaviours.

How can we learn more about ourselves through brain science? We need to start by looking at our brains and how we process information – the stimulus of life. I am going to focus on how our brain impacts on how we show up in life. (I apologise up front to any neuroscientists reading this for my simplified version of brain functions.)

Our brain has three parts to it:

- brain stem, or reptilian brain
- limbic brain, or mammalian brain
- the neocortex, or human brain.

Let's have a look at these.

Brain stem or reptilian brain

In evolutionary terms this is the oldest part of our brain, and we share how this part operates with all other animals that have a brain. This collection of neurons makes sure our body functions systematically; it controls breathing, circulation and so on. This part of the brain has no ability to 'think' – it is completely responsive.

Limbic brain or mammalian brain

The limbic brain is responsible for all feelings, such as happiness, trust and loyalty. It is also responsible for all human behaviour and decision making, yet it has no capacity for language.

We often make choices to do or not do things based on our emotions. We may claim that we have been rational, but in reality in most cases we resort to what we believe 'feels right' or we go with our 'gut feeling' or our intuition. All these senses sit in the limbic or emotional part of the brain and are at the core of the choices we make in life.

The oldest part of the limbic brain is the amygdala, which controls the fight or flight response that keeps us out of danger. Amygdala conditions such as anxiety, depression and phobias are also known to be linked to abnormal functioning of the amygdala, owing to damage, developmental problems or neurotransmitter imbalance.

The neocortex or human brain

The neocortex is the newest part of the brain. Although all mammals have this part of the brain, a large and developed neocortex is uniquely human. It is responsible for all rational and analytical thought, speech and language.

The neocortex is the only thinking part of our brain. It is always trying to understand and make sense of the world. Asking questions about a feeling converts it from a feeling to a thought. When we can go beyond expressing what we feel about something to rationally explaining what sits behind that feeling we have pushed our thinking into the neocortex. When we push our feelings to become thoughts we can make sense of their meaning.

Human brain (neocortex)
Higher order thinking

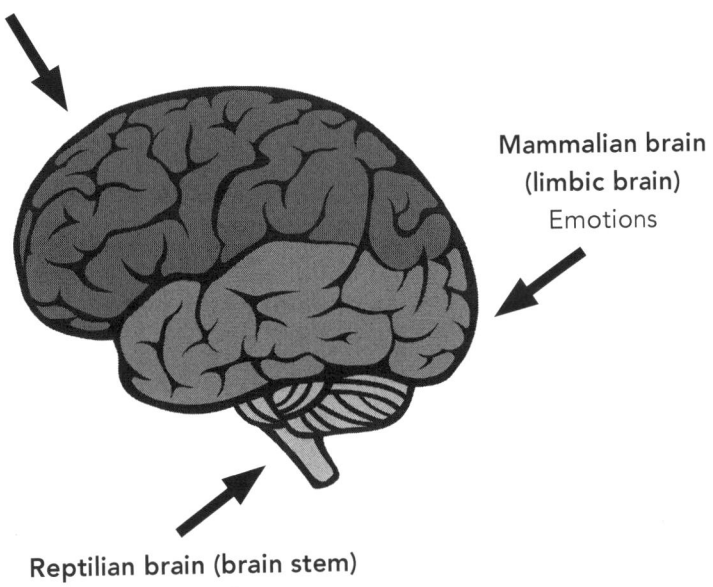

**Mammalian brain
(limbic brain)**
Emotions

Reptilian brain (brain stem)
Survival

> 'Be yourself. Everyone else is taken.'
>
> **Oscar Wilde**

The power of understanding how our brain works, and the physiology behind it, is that we can harness that understanding to make more sense of our own thoughts and feelings, and also in some cases even more importantly understand how these brain triggers are impacting how other people around us appear to us. Through understanding brain function and its link to behaviour, trust me – the world around you will become more interesting and start to make more sense!

Sparks and Jolts

Who am I?

TO LOOK FORWARD IN LIFE, FIRST REFLECT ON WHERE YOU'VE BEEN

To project forward our life and design it, first we need to look back and see what has defined our life experience to date. The common life stages from childhood to teenager to adulthood to parent to caregiver are real and different for all of us, and each life chapter shaped or changed us in some way. These life chapters give us a great window into who we really are and how we navigate our world. Initially you may brush events off as a set of random situations that have no interrelationship with each other, but look a bit deeper and patterns start to emerge. Every aspect of our life to date has shaped us in some way. How we show up now, today, is impacted good or bad by our life journey to date. That *is* life!

> 'Life is not about how fast you run or high you climb but how well you bounce.'
>
> **Tigger (A.A. Milne)**

Highs and lows are a fact of life

Life is a series of highs and lows. From coaching the amazing people I coach I find that many feel that other people's lives are less troubled with less juggling and chaos than their own – they are the 'messed up' one! Trust me, this is *not* the case. I have found everyone – and I mean *everyone* – has had things happen to them that have impacted them, good and bad – things they've achieved, failures they've encountered, devastating tragedies or loss they have endured, relationship challenges and highlights, crises of confidence, periods of work stress, and major highs. Each encounter, experience and emotion is an embedded part of our Life Fingerprint. It's part of us, and each situation and how we reacted to it was a manifestation of who we really are.

Don't compare your life to other people's highlight reels

> 'The reason we struggle with insecurity is because we compare our behind-the-scenes with everyone else's highlight reel.'
>
> **Steven Furtick**

The challenge is we often compare our behind-the-scenes uncut version of our life that only we know with everyone else's external portrayal of their life, so it should be no surprise other people's highly edited external summary looks way more together, exciting and rewarding than our own life, because people publicly share the main highlights but skim over the low lights. Yet even knowing this we often can't help but compare the highlight reel of their best moments with our raw and uncut version that only we know. Research has shown that social media such as Facebook has increased the levels of life dissatisfaction and in some cases depression. The steady stream of photos and posts of great dinners out, social get togethers and holiday pics is the highlight reel of other people's lives, and subconsciously it can make our everyday life with its ups and downs seem not that exciting ... but just see that for what it is – 'the best bits' – and focus your attention back on yourself and what really matters to you. Everybody has the same issues that you do. Everybody.

THE DARK SIDE OF NOT BEING WHO YOU REALLY ARE ...

This book was created out of a belief that everyone, and I mean *every-one*, can create and live their best life. My own inspiration was the goal of best life creation, but the more people I meet and coach the more I realise that so many people – too many people – feel they can't fully be themselves. They can't define who they really are, and as a result aren't feeling like they are living up to their potential.

Many people at some point feel unhappy, unsettled, and rather lost if they can't define themselves and truly be themselves. Beyond feeling unhappy, many feel stressed, in some cases to the point of depression. The signs can be subtle: not feeling confident, or feelings of self-doubt. Many have had their confidence knocked by other people, particularly those close to them such as their family, partner or boss. For many of the people I coach, particularly women, it can be exhausting feeling like you can't truly be yourself and be respected for it. For many it is the result of being told they are too *something* ... too passionate, too collaborative, too ideas based, too idealistic, too whatever the other person thinks they are. This judgement is a silent killer of people's hopes, dreams and confidence. (In subsequent chapters we will explore this more.)

Whether driven by inspiration or desperation, thinking, planning and living your life can work. Defining your **Who** will allow you to fully be yourself versus trying to be someone else. Accepting that who you are is enough ... for both you and others. You will find and discover your Life Fingerprint versus being a Life Chameleon. It's about you doing this for yourself, but then letting others be themselves too.

> 'If you tell the truth, you don't have to remember anything.'
>
> **Mark Twain**

JOINING THE LIFE DOTS THROUGH SYNTHESIS

There are three exercises I've put together that help you start the Synthesis of **Who** you really are and examine the reality of how you currently show up in life. They are:

- Life Line

- Values

- Strengths.

They were composed to help you take stock of where you are now versus your life to date, and provide the foundation for subsequently finding the patterns and Synergy to start to discover **Who** you are.

SYNTHESIS: LIFE LINE EXERCISE

The reason I always start Life Design with a Life Line exercise is that our life so far is a window into what our future Life Design should be. The patterns of our life start at an incredibly early age, with our Life Fingerprint already started when we are born. We've already been dealt a genetic set of cards through what we inherited from our parents, and over time we decide how we play these cards.

Every experience we go through, whether it is a high or a low, shapes us in some way because it invokes feelings in us. Many of those feelings we ignore as not important, but when we really reflect on our Life Line they pop back up again. They may have been hidden from view and kept in a box, but they are real, present and shaping how we think, feel and act – whether we acknowledge it or not. Of all the exercises, this first one is the most powerful if you really immerse yourself in it. I will warn you it will make you think and reflect, but trust me – that is a good thing.

Over the following pages you will see a simple Life Line exercise. The x axis is time, the y axis is the magnitude of the high and low. You can either complete the exercise in the book or draw the same axes on a piece of paper – starting from the earliest point in your life that is meaningful to you – and steadily mark up the highs and lows. Then, for each of them, reflect in the table not only on what was going on but why that was a high or low for you.

On pages 40 and 41 I've included some examples to get you thinking, but that's only a guide. Think through your own. Give yourself some space and time to do it. Put an hour aside somewhere quiet and by yourself and give it a go. If you read on at this point, don't leave it too long before doing this exercise, because you will get much more from the rest of the book having done it. Given this book is all about *you*, this is where you should start.

The Life Line exercise, although very simple, is very powerful in terms of what comes out of it … just do it and you will see.

LIFE LINE EXERCISE

- Thinking of your life to date, starting at the earliest point that is meaningful to you, write in the graphs on pages 42–45 what you feel have been the high and low points. Don't overthink it – just go with your intuition on how you felt.

- Do a quick first pass to get out the major points, focusing on the big highs and big lows. Then add other significant events. Include observations about both work and your personal life.

- You should spend at least an hour reflecting on this. Your first draft should come quickly, but stick with it longer to ensure you are thinking deeply about all major events and how they made you feel.

- Reflect on what defined the highs and the lows and capture them in the summary pages.

Life Line example

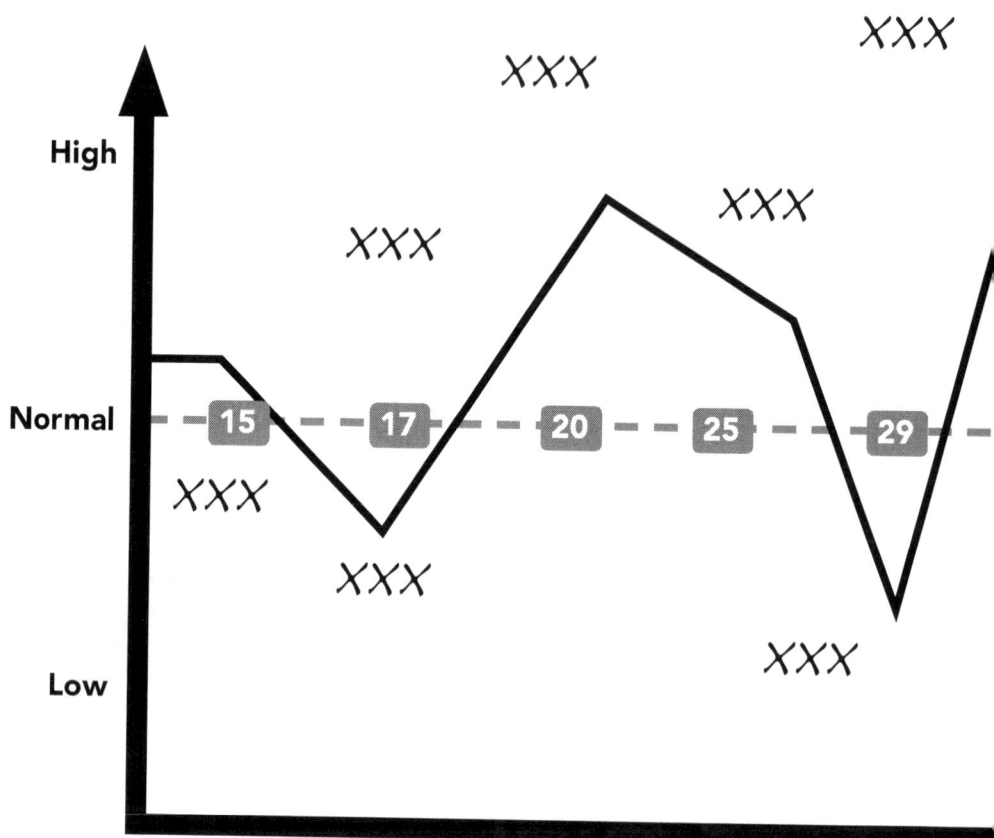

Time in years (focus on highs and lows)

LIFE LINE

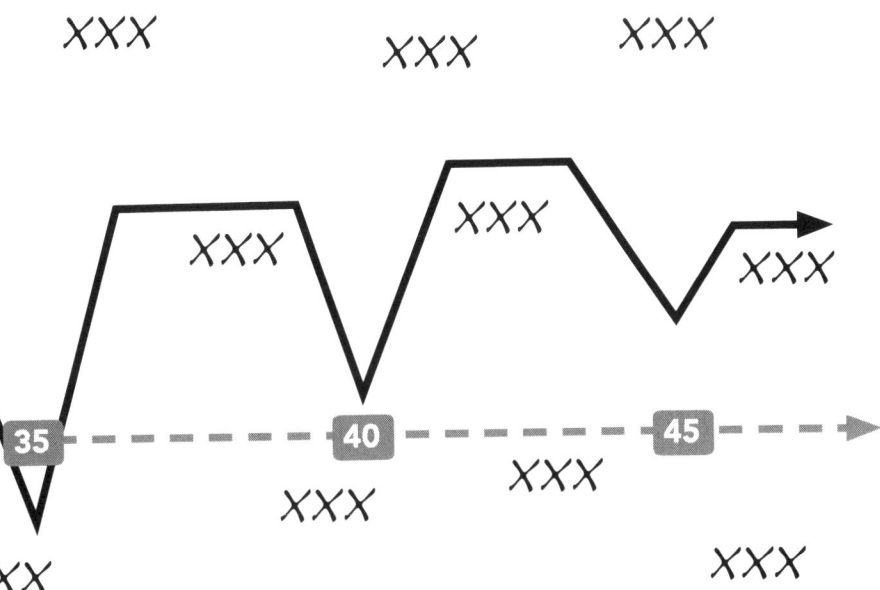

Life Line example

... from other people who have completed the exercise.

Highs

- Job I loved
- Relationships and key milestone events (friends, family, partner, kids)
- Good bosses
- Achievements (school, uni, work)
- Learning something
- A moment I made a difference
- Freedom and independence
- How someone made me feel (praise, support, etc.)
- Travel
- Spiritual
- Hobbies and interests
- Great living environment

Lows

- Jobs I didn't like
- Relationships and key milestone events (friends, family, partner, kids)
- Bad work culture
- Bad bosses
- Health issues (me or others)
- Stress or depression
- Lack of purpose or achievement
- Financial worries
- How someone made me feel (bullying, negative relationships, etc.)
- Poor living environment

Thinking of your life to date, starting at the earliest point that is meaningful to you, write in what you feel have been the high and low points. Don't overthink it – just go with your intuition on how you felt.

Do a first draft of your Life Line. Do this quickly.

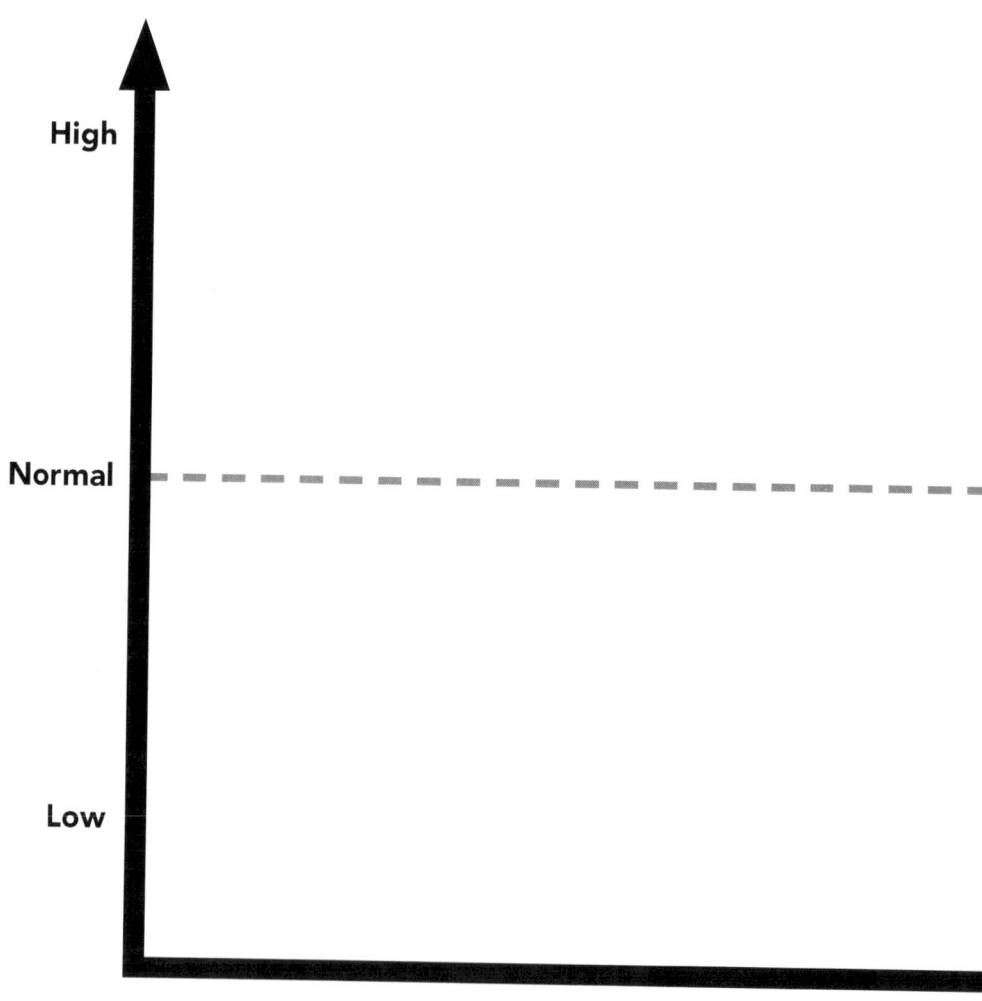

Time in years (focus on highs and lows)

LIFE LINE

Now complete the exercise again, thinking deeply about all major events and how they made you feel.

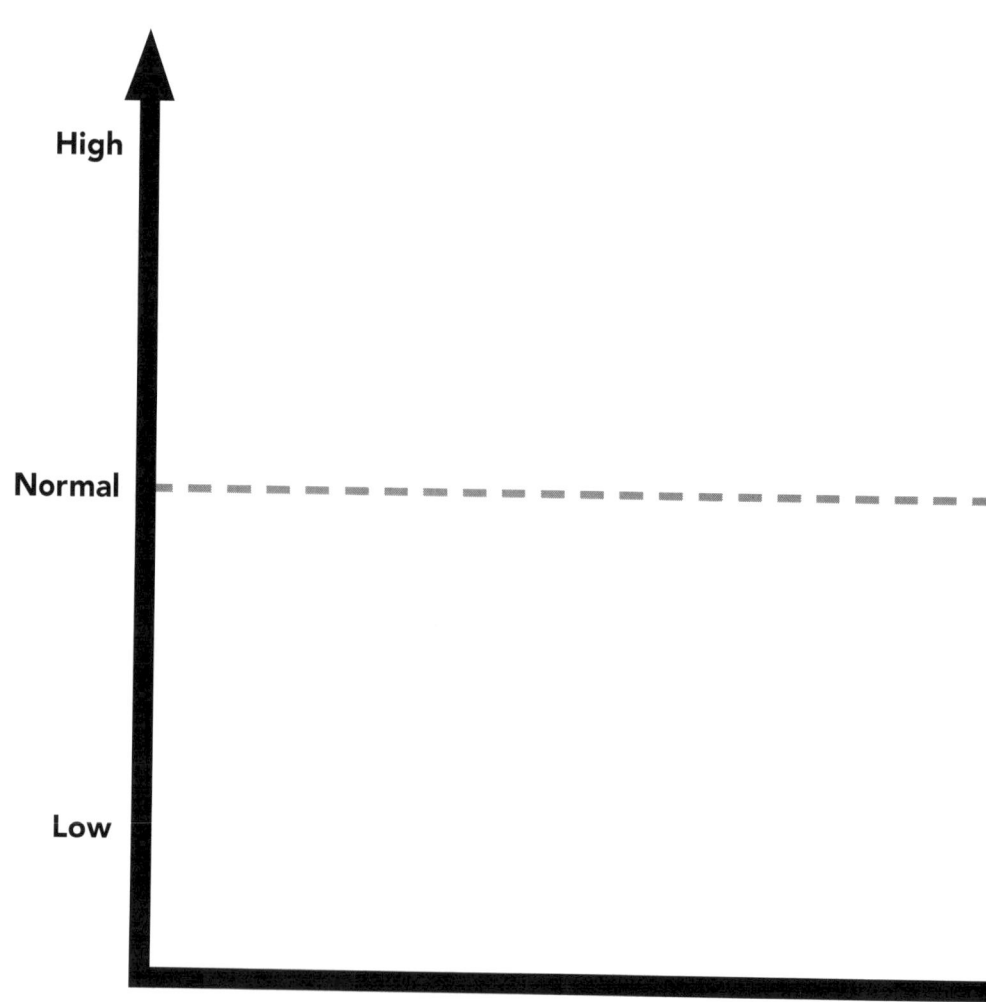

High

Normal

Low

Time in years (focus on highs and lows)

LIFE LINE

Reflect on what defined the highs and capture your thoughts here.

Highs

What defined the highs and why?

Lows

_____

_____

_____

_____

_____

_____

_____

_____

_____

_____

_____

_____

_____

_____

What defined the lows and why?

SYNTHESIS: VALUES EXERCISE

Defining and being clear on your values is another key part of the Life Design jigsaw. Our values define who we are and how we navigate our life – they are our compass. You may feel you are clear on your values already, but if – like many others – you have a rough idea but are not totally sure, this exercise will really help. In the following pages is a list of values. Read this list and tick the relevant column according to how important each value is to you. Once complete, read back through the list and double check they feel right.

> 'Real integrity is doing the right thing, knowing that nobody's going to know whether you did it or not.'
>
> **Oprah Winfrey**

Then look back over your very important values and decide on your top five most important values. Spend some time reflecting on why these five are so important to you. Capture your thoughts in the summary pages provided. How do you feel? Are you currently living your life by the value priorities you have chosen? Also think about what's really not important at all to you. Capture any further thoughts in the notes pages.

SORTING OUT WHAT YOU VALUE

- Your values are the things that are most important to you; the beliefs and ideas that guide you in your life. Your values should be the foundation of your personal vision and purpose in your personal life and in work.

- Being aware of your values not only helps you make decisions about your work and life but also helps you understand what situations bring out the best in you.

- This exercise helps you sort through your values and your personal success criteria. It also enables you to prioritise your values so that you are equally clear on those that are important to you and those that are not.

- Allow a minimum of one hour to sort through the values and rank them in importance, and take more time if you need it to reflect and capture your thoughts on the five values that are most important to you.

Step 1: For each of the values listed in the following pages, tick the relevant column according to how important each value is to you. For example, if Achievement is very important to you then tick 'Very important'. Continue down the list, ticking the box that most accurately describes each value's importance to you.

Step 2: Look at your 'Very important' values. Which ones jump out at you? Asterisk your stand-out values.

Step 3: Choose the five most important values from those you have just asterisked from your 'Very important' values and write them on pages 58 and 59, and capture why each value is so important to you.

	Not important	Important	Very important
ACHIEVEMENT To have important accomplishments	☐	☐	☐
ADVENTURE To have new and exciting experiences	☐	☐	☐
AESTHETICS The appreciation of art and the beauty of things around me	☐	☐	☐
AUTHENTICITY Being able to just be myself	☐	☐	☐
AUTHORITY To be in charge of and responsible for others	☐	☐	☐
AUTONOMY To be self-determined and independent	☐	☐	☐
BOSS To work for someone I trust and respect	☐	☐	☐
CHALLENGE To take on difficult tasks and problems	☐	☐	☐
CHANGE To have a life full of change and variety	☐	☐	☐
COLLEAGUES To work with others I like and respect	☐	☐	☐
COMFORT To have a pleasant and comfortable life	☐	☐	☐
COMMUNITY To be involved in my community	☐	☐	☐
COMPASSION The desire to help others who are suffering	☐	☐	☐
CONTRIBUTION To make a lasting contribution in the world	☐	☐	☐

VALUES

	Not important	Important	Very important
COOPERATION To work collaboratively with others	☐	☐	☐
CREATIVITY To have new and original ideas	☐	☐	☐
DIGNITY All people should be treated well and given space to be their best	☐	☐	☐
DUTY To carry out my duties and obligations	☐	☐	☐
ECOLOGY To live in harmony with the environment	☐	☐	☐
EXCITEMENT To have a life full of excitement and stimulation	☐	☐	☐
FAIRNESS To navigate life through what is right and wrong, fair or unfair	☐	☐	☐
FAME To be well known and recognised	☐	☐	☐
FAMILY To have a happy, loving family	☐	☐	☐
FINANCIAL SECURITY To feel I have what I need	☐	☐	☐
FITNESS To be physically fit and strong	☐	☐	☐
FLEXIBILITY To adjust to new circumstances easily	☐	☐	☐
FRIENDSHIP To have close, supportive friends	☐	☐	☐
FUN To play and have fun	☐	☐	☐

VALUES

	Not important	Important	Very important
GENEROSITY To give what I have to others	☐	☐	☐
GENUINENESS To act in a manner that is true to who I am	☐	☐	☐
GROWTH To keep changing and growing	☐	☐	☐
HARMONY To connect humanity and the natural world together sustainably	☐	☐	☐
HEALTH To be physically well and healthy	☐	☐	☐
HONESTY To be honest and truthful	☐	☐	☐
HUMOUR To see the humorous side of myself and the world	☐	☐	☐
INDEPENDENCE To be free from dependence on others	☐	☐	☐
INTEGRITY Being honest and true to myself	☐	☐	☐
INTERESTS AND HOBBIES To spend time pursuing my interests	☐	☐	☐
KNOWLEDGE To learn and contribute valuable knowledge	☐	☐	☐
LEISURE To take time to relax and enjoy	☐	☐	☐
LOVED To be loved by those close to me	☐	☐	☐

VALUES

	Not important	Important	Very important
LOVING To give love to others	☐	☐	☐
MASTERY To be competent in my everyday activities	☐	☐	☐
NON-CONFORMITY To question and challenge authority and norms	☐	☐	☐
OPENNESS To be open to new experiences, ideas and options	☐	☐	☐
OPTIMISM To feel and believe anything is possible if you apply yourself to it	☐	☐	☐
ORDER To have a life that is well-ordered and organised	☐	☐	☐
PASSION To have deep feelings about ideas, activities or people	☐	☐	☐
POPULARITY To be well liked by many people	☐	☐	☐
POWER To have control over others	☐	☐	☐
PURPOSE To have meaning and direction in my life	☐	☐	☐
RATIONALITY To be guided by reason and logic	☐	☐	☐
REALISM To see and act realistically and practically	☐	☐	☐
RESPONSIBILITY To make and carry out responsible decisions	☐	☐	☐

VALUES

	Not important	Important	Very important
RISK To take risks and chances	☐	☐	☐
SELF-IMAGE To feel others respect me	☐	☐	☐
SIMPLICITY To live life simply, with minimal needs	☐	☐	☐
SOLITUDE To have time and space where I can be apart from others	☐	☐	☐
SPIRITUALITY To grow and mature spiritually	☐	☐	☐
STABILITY To have a life that stays fairly consistent	☐	☐	☐
TEACH To share knowledge and experience to help others grow	☐	☐	☐
THINKING To have space and time to reflect on my thoughts and ideas	☐	☐	☐
TOGETHERNESS To have a sense of belonging to something greater than myself	☐	☐	☐
TOLERANCE To live and let live	☐	☐	☐
TRAVEL To explore and visit new places and cultures	☐	☐	☐
WEALTH To have plenty of money	☐	☐	☐
WISDOM Sharing my experience, knowledge and experience with others	☐	☐	☐

VALUES

Notes

Look at your 'Very important' values. Which ones jump out at you? Asterisk your stand-out values.

Choose the five most important values from those you have just asterisked from your 'Very important' values and write them here, and capture why each value is so important to you.

My top five Values

1

2

VALUES

3

4

5

SYNTHESIS: DEFINING YOUR STRENGTHS

An increasing number of scientific studies have shown that people achieve greater positive improvements in their performance by building on their strengths compared to addressing their weaknesses. The reason is our strengths tend to come more naturally to us and are more intuitive. If we focus on amplifying these strengths we not only enhance our performance but we also derive greater satisfaction from jobs and experiences that utilise our strengths.

DEFINING YOUR STRENGTHS

- This exercise will help you think through your strengths and assess to what degree you operate within each strength. The exercise will also enable you to be equally clear on those areas where you don't feel as comfortable; these will be development areas.

- Allow a minimum of one hour to assess your strengths, and take more time if you need it at the end to reflect and capture your thoughts on the five strengths that you think are most important to you.

Step 1: For each of the strengths listed in the following pages, tick the relevant column according to how relevant each strength is to you. For example, if Achiever is very important to you then tick 'Key strength'. Continue down the list, ticking the box that most accurately describes this strength for you. Go through the exercise intuitively to start with. Once complete, read through it and adjust your responses if needed so that they are a true reflection of you.

Step 2: Choose your top five strengths from the 'Key strength' column and write them on pages 64 and 65, and capture why each is a strength for you. When you use it, how does it help you achieve more?

STRENGTHS

	DEVELOPING/ GAP (Not my preferred operating approach)	SUPPORTING STRENGTH (I do operate in this area to a similar level to others)	KEY STRENGTH (My preferred intuitive approach)
ACHIEVER Determined to achieve goals, overcome obstacles	☐	☐	☐
ADAPTIVE Adapt and sense what needs to be done to stay on track	☐	☐	☐
ANALYTICAL Come at problems through analysis first	☐	☐	☐
ARRANGER Mobilise what's needed to make something happen	☐	☐	☐
BIG PICTURE See the bigger picture/context of issues and opportunities	☐	☐	☐
COLLABORATIVE Get things done by engaging with others	☐	☐	☐
CONNECTED Like to work in connection with other people	☐	☐	☐
CONSISTENT Fair and objective in taking on new challenges and in the treatment of others	☐	☐	☐
CREATIVE Come at problems in a different way to other people	☐	☐	☐
CURIOUS Intrigued by how things work, or how things can be improved	☐	☐	☐
DECISIVE Make decisions on time and move forward with certainty	☐	☐	☐

STRENGTHS

	DEVELOPING/ GAP (Not my preferred operating approach)	SUPPORTING STRENGTH (I do operate in this area to a similar level to others)	KEY STRENGTH (My preferred intuitive approach)
DEPENDABLE Reliable and dependable contributor to projects, preferring being behind the scenes versus fronting up a project	☐	☐	☐
DEVELOPER Take ideas and translate them into practical solutions	☐	☐	☐
DEVELOPING OTHERS Invest in development and building the potential of others	☐	☐	☐
DOER Practical and 'hands on'	☐	☐	☐
ENERGETIC Immerses themselves in projects with energy	☐	☐	☐
INCLUSIVE Form teams with different kinds of people/different strengths	☐	☐	☐
INDIVIDUAL Get results through own personal focus and individual drive vs team approach	☐	☐	☐
INNOVATIVE See new ways to do things; enjoy coming up with new things	☐	☐	☐
INTELLECTUAL Thrive on thinking things through from different angles	☐	☐	☐
INTERPERSONAL Build and develop projects through relationships with others	☐	☐	☐
INVENTIVE Create new inventions	☐	☐	☐

STRENGTHS

	DEVELOPING/ GAP (Not my preferred operating approach)	SUPPORTING STRENGTH (I do operate in this area to a similar level to others)	KEY STRENGTH (My preferred intuitive approach)
LEARNER Seek to always be learning new things	☐	☐	☐
PERSPECTIVE Keep sight and perspective on the bigger picture	☐	☐	☐
POSITIVITY Can see possibilities of what can be achieved, and also instils this in others	☐	☐	☐
PRACTICAL Adaptive and pragmatic	☐	☐	☐
RESPONSIBILITY Take the lead in getting things done; keep to project commitments	☐	☐	☐
RESULTS ORIENTED Goal directed, strives to get the result	☐	☐	☐
RISK TAKING Weigh up pros and cons and comfortable taking risks to accelerate progress	☐	☐	☐
SENSING Intrigued by what motivates other people to behave as they do	☐	☐	☐
STRATEGIC Enjoy strategic thinking and joining the dots	☐	☐	☐
SYSTEMS THINKER Think long term and holistically	☐	☐	☐
TEAM BASED Get results through mobilising and engaging others	☐	☐	☐

STRENGTHS

Choose five strengths from the 'Key strength' column and write them below, and capture why each one is a strength for you. When you use it, how does it help you achieve more?

My top five Strengths

1
_____

_____

_____

_____

_____

2
_____

_____

_____

_____

_____

3

4

5

LOOKING FOR CLUES IN YOUR LIFE LINE, VALUES AND STRENGTHS

Now you have completed the first three exercises in Life Design, I am sure some patterns and observations about your life, your values and your strengths will be starting to emerge for you.

One area I discovered in myself, and have found in all of the people I've coached and is a universal truth: big clues to our Life Fingerprint were visible in our childhood. How we showed up as a child and the many patterns of interests, strengths, values, experiences and relationships reappear and repeat throughout our life. Did you find this when you did the exercises?

You may have also discovered through these exercises that certain circumstances or emotions prompt a particular response from you.

As you self-coach yourself through each of the exercises and stages of Life Design, try to spot patterns in your behaviours, in your feelings and in your actions. Doing so becomes an interesting and important part of the self-learning journey, and something that you will become more adept at the more you practise.

To act as further stimulus to your thoughts, I wanted to share some ideas that I hope will get you thinking about how they apply to you. They are in four areas:

- Maslow's hierarchy of needs

- examining your hot buttons

- discovering your triggers

- understanding your self-esteem.

Examining your motivations and who you are

Abraham Maslow conducted an amazing study published in a 1943 paper, 'A Theory of Human Motivation', in the *Psychological Review*. This study is the bedrock of many sociology and psychology studies since, and many later studies have further built on this foundational understanding. This work (shown in the diagram on the following page) explains most patterns of behaviour, and it is still the foundation of studies into human motivations today.

Maslow's hierarchy of needs

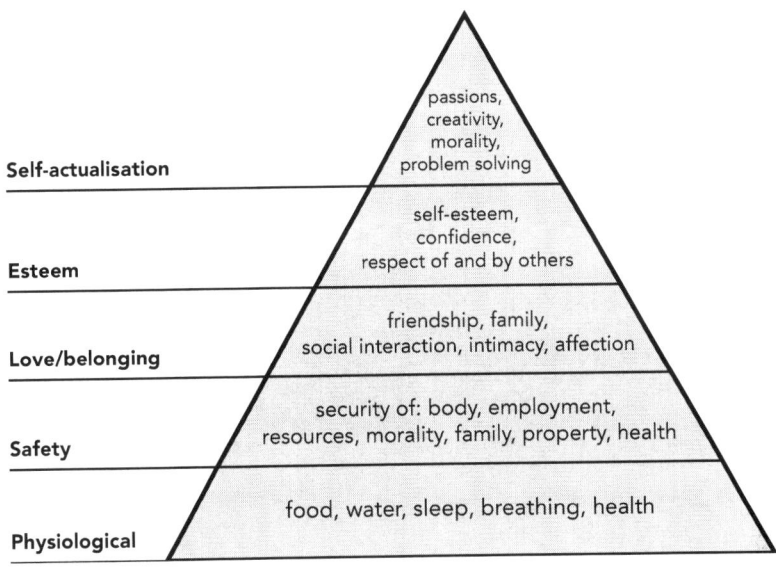

Understanding who we are through the lens of human motivations is at the core of understanding who we are individually.

It is also incredibly important for how we set about creating work environments and work ecosystems that ensure our motivation needs are met. Conducted in 2015 by The Energy Project in association with *Harvard Business Review*, a survey of 20,000 people found: 'Deriving a sense of meaning and significance from their work had the highest single impact of any variable in the survey. Employees who did find meaning in their work also reported being 2.8 times more likely to stay with their organization, 2.2 times more satisfied with their jobs, and 93% more engaged.'

We will return to this thought when we explore **What**.

ACTION: What does this mean to me?

Look for linkages between motivations and Life Design and values. How did your need for love and belonging appear as a high or low or in your values? How is confidence and self-esteem playing out ?

Reflect any observations you make in the exercise.

Examining your hot buttons

If you look at the highs and lows of your Life Line or simply how you react to everyday situations and compare these with your top 5 values, you should start to see correlations emerging. The Highs tend to correlate with us living our values and playing to our strengths; the lows on the other hand link to times when we have felt our values may have been challenged. When you examine your hot buttons of what triggers a negative reaction in you, you should see a linkage to your values, because our values are a core part of our belief system in our Who. Looking specifically at the values that tend to be more evident in how we work, I have clustered them into typical groupings below. See which ones are most similar to you.

Integrity = authenticity, genuine, honesty, integrity, contribution

In charge = authority, power

Certain = order, stability, comfort

Independent = flexibility, autonomy, wisdom, independence, mastery, thinking

Flex = change, creativity, growth, non-conformity, risk

Equal = dignity, fairness, tolerance

Collaborative = co-operation, compassion, harmony, collaboration

When our values are challenged, our behaviour related to this is one of reacting to a perceived threat. To our mammalian ancestors the triggers of a threat response were more external environmental factors such as fear of predators and being eaten. In humans the threats have evolved significantly, and the threat is now often a threat to who we are, but interestingly it still creates a threat response and an amygdala reaction of fight or flight in the same way because you feel like you are in danger.

Our own reactions and those of others we know and work with can be mapped back to reactions to a threat to our values. Once we understand these patterns, it can help us realise the core concerns of others and of ourselves when we perceive a threat in these areas. Each of us has a predominant trigger; once we understand what it is we can think through what style or approach works best to get the most out of ourselves or others.

Once you understand the triggers of your own behaviour, that of others becomes much clearer and easier to understand. Some typical examples of each behaviour in others are:

- **Integrity:** They will apply this value in both their work and interactions with others; they may be triggered by others who don't share that value, especially if they expect them to do something they believe to be dishonest or not genuine. If others accused them of doing something such as being misleading or lying, this accusation would trigger a feeling of an attack on their integrity.

- **In charge**: If a person is driven by being 'in charge', they want to lead and drive thinking or decision making – or both – and seek to be in control; they may be triggered by challenge and questioning, and see this as an attack on their authority, and they will react badly to challenges from others who are lower down the 'pecking order' than they are.

- **Certain:** People who need certainty find uncertainty a threat or trigger. They will react badly to ambiguity, to open-ended project briefs, to lack of clarity about whose job it is to do something, and will feel uneasy when the goal posts shift.

- **Independent:** These people don't like to be boxed in and constrained. They like a free run to think independently and make choices about how they do things, and want the freedom to act in the way they feel is right versus following norms or consensus. They can be triggered by being made to comply with a way of doing something, or by traditional structures and hierarchies.

- **Flex:** These people seek change and variety, and like to leave projects more open ended to leave space for new ideas and creativity. They like to have an open remit to try new things and take risks in the pursuit of an even better idea or solution. They can be triggered by deadlines or process, feeling that these constrain them and crush their creativity.

- **Equal:** They have a strong sense of what they regard as fair or unfair in relation to how people are treated. They will feel uncomfortable and triggered if people are disadvantaged by a decision; they will be the voice of others who may not be at the table. They will stand up for the inclusion of others. If somebody has agreed to something and then backtracks from that agreement, they will be triggered to seek to uphold the decision.

- **Collaborative:** These people are in tune with how other people are thinking and feeling about a situation. They seek to ensure others are heard. They show high trust and loyalty to others, and are triggered by pressure to take the credit or do it themselves when they believe doing it with others is the answer. They also are triggered by a successful collaboration breaking down, if trust is broken.

Each of us has a different radar and hot buttons for what our triggers are; hopefully from these examples you will be starting to form a picture on your own triggers.

To practise your ability to spot the triggers, you can start to observe others based on the clusters outlined. Some interesting dynamics I have observed in meetings include the tensions between a team member wanting certainty and needing to know when and how something should be done versus a person who seeks independence who may be fine to agree on what needs to be done but refuses to commit to doing it a certain way. In charge leaders can trigger reactions in collaborative team members who seek to ensure everyone is heard regardless of status or age or seniority, and to build decisions in collaboration. In-charge–driven leaders act with the belief that asking other people is unduly wasting time when they have the answers and authority to just make a call. This dynamic can result in In-charge-driven leaders dismissing collaborative leaders as weak because they won't just make the call; on the other hand collaborative leaders often regard In-charge leaders as arrogant and unwilling to listen.

From this idea, start to make observations about your own triggers and those of people at work in the trigger page (page 73).

ACTION: What does this mean to me?

Capture any observations you make on your 'hot buttons' and triggers and add to your notes in Life Line and Values.

Discovering your triggers

If you have realised you are in a negative loop with your own triggers and hot buttons, the first step in escaping it is recognising it. Our triggers often invoke thoughts and feelings about ourselves that we need to pay close attention to. If we ignore them we do so at our peril, because feelings, funnily enough, are how we feel about ourselves and our place in the world. If we ignore them or suppress them we are in effect turning our backs on ourselves. Or to put it another way, if you were having a conversation with a close friend and you could see they were troubled about something, a bit upset or a bit emotional, you would stay in the conversation and try to understand, listen and hear them. You should show the same care and compassion to yourself. I am not recommending a full 'out loud' conversation – just pause for a minute or two when you see that you have been triggered.

Take a typical example: someone says something to you and you feel yourself reacting – it invokes a feeling in you. This time, instead of ignoring it or brushing it off (which is a normal response), stick with it for a minute or two after the event, and try to work through what the feeling really made you feel, and then what its trigger was. The steps are:

- **Event happens:** Someone makes a comment; maybe they say something about you or your work, say something about your project or say something about your team. Let the event happen, then soon afterwards reflect and gather your thoughts.

- **What happened there?** They said this, then this.

- **What reaction did it create in my body?** My heart rate has gone up; I feel like I'm getting hot; I feel like I'm blushing; I can feel myself getting angry; I can feel myself getting upset, I feel I may cry …

- **How did it make me feel?** Challenged, under threat, attacked, nervous, anxious, upset.

- **Why did those comments make me react?** *Feel* through (compared to our normal approach of '*think* through') which apply to you; it's important to feel these and not think about them in a rational way because that's where the insight lies: they challenged my integrity; they weren't listening; they thought my work was bad;

I let them down; I did something to provoke them; they don't like me; they were attacking my team; they were being mean to my friend …

- **Write down your conclusions.** Now compare your conclusions to your list of important values and strengths we captured in earlier exercises. In most cases our emotional reactions link directly back to challenging who we are. Examples of triggers are:
  - someone says you are lying and you have integrity as a key value – this is a trigger
  - someone makes comments such as, 'Did you think of this?' or 'Did you try that?' If you are a perfectionist – this is a trigger
  - someone keeps challenging another team member and you value fairness and sharing perspectives – this is a trigger.

ACTION: What are your triggers?

You may already know what they are intuitively; if not, just conduct this simple exercise over a couple of weeks and see what pops up (you can jot these down on the following page). You will usually end up with two to five triggers, and once you know what they are you can work on tackling them. Reflect on your values: often if people challenge your values it can be a source for a trigger, and also these same triggers if sustained will appear as a low on your Life Line.

What triggers you? How do you react? What would you like to do differently now you know it's a trigger?

Understanding your confidence and self-esteem

Linked to these observations about how we react and what our triggers are, one aspect of Life Design that I have found can be debilitating for people is always trying to impress others or seeking to feel validated, seeking approval versus being good with ourselves, being concerned about what other people think of us versus what I think of myself.

In coaching, I find that so many people's self-esteem is tied up with other people's perceptions of them. Other people are of course significant in our lives and we want to have good relationships with others, but having self-esteem so tied up in what others think can be exhausting: your boss, your partner, your kids, your parents and your peers have the power, through what they say, to take your self-esteem away. The other option is you owning it. Owning it means you know in your gut that what you do is valuable, and although you care about other people's perceptions of you because that helps you understand how you build a relationship with them, it cannot alone determine your self-esteem, because you know you are good enough.

> 'Keep away from people who try to belittle your ambitions. Small people always do that, but the really great make you feel that you, too, can become great.'
>
> **Mark Twain**

If I look at myself as an example, to others at work I came across as self-assured and confident and always there for them, however my own self-rating showed that I felt defined by what others thought of me. My feeling of value was directly linked to my perceived contribution to others, versus me being able to clearly see for myself my intrinsic value and to regard myself as valuable. This might sound like a small reframe, but for me it was massive – doing something that I see as valuable means I can self-assess, but being valued by others takes others to validate me. In reality I still seek to be valuable by helping others – that is my purpose – but now I trust my instincts to tell me if I'm on the right path, versus needing validation and reassurance from others to tell me that. This was all part of my journey to being good at being me … but it's also a work in progress, and always will be!

I find people's lack of confidence and self-esteem challenges often stem from doing things not aligned with who they are. You know it because you feel it, but then you rationally try to work it out ... it must be me ... I'm not thinking straight ... it must be something I said or did or am ...

It's not that. You are you, but in such situations you don't feel good about yourself.

My nature is to do my best. I am a recovering perfectionist, and when I give something my all, I do like to know I made a difference. If I feel my efforts fall short of that bar I can't help myself from being my own worst critic. This is a problem that still shows up for me now and then.

This is the loop I see so many of my clients stuck in at work, and if this loop is repeated day in, day out, it is tiring, unfulfilling and unengaging. A better loop is: *I know what I am passionate about. I know my values. I am proud of my strengths or gifts, and those parts of me combined mean I know my purpose. I choose to follow my instinct into a job, a career or an entrepreneurial path that is totally 100% me and totally congruent with who I am. Every day I feel passionate about what I do. I enjoy it, and I feel what I do is valuable. I am now happy, because I am me and being me is valuable.*

Wouldn't you love to be in this positive loop?

ACTION: How does your level of self-esteem and confidence impact you?

Looking at both your Life Line and Strengths through the lens of self-esteem and confidence can provide additional insight. If you reflect back, how closely do your highs and lows reflect the impact of confidence? How does it impact on how you see your strengths?

Notes

NOTES

MY JOURNEY TO DISCOVER MY <u>WHO</u>

What I realised, particularly from my Life Line exercise, is that unravelling who I really am and subsequently how that showed up in what I enjoy doing revealed a winding path to where I am now. I won't share all the inner secrets of my Life Line, but I will share one example that surprised and encouraged me. As you read it I hope you will find it interesting, but that's not why I've included it: I want you to think about just early memories and what they may mean for how you show up now and who you really are.

Being a work and life anthropologist

In later chapters I will share more about my own influencers along my path, but let me now explore one of the most significant people to have influenced me: Sir David Attenborough. 'But this is a business and self-help book,' I hear you cry, 'Where is she going with this David Attenborough thing?'

Don't worry – all will become clear.

> 'If you are always trying to be normal you will never know how amazing you can be.'
>
> **Maya Angelou**

When Sir David Attenborough's *Life on Earth* series was first shown on television in 1979 I was 11 years old. Through that amazing nature program filmed deep in rainforests and jungles, on the tops of mountains and beneath vast oceans, my lens on the world changed forever. For those of you who didn't grow up with the program, it was a chronological natural history lesson of life on Earth, from the simplest life forms to primates.

Through those Sunday-night hourly immersions, I felt I had a new window to the world opened up to me. At age 11, I was living in the UK, in the medieval town of Salisbury (but at that age, trust me, living somewhere small, pretty and historic was not that exciting, though going back now to visit I really appreciate it). I had never been overseas; in fact, I had never been on holiday anywhere other than my grandparents' house. My lens on the world was narrow, shaped only at that age by my parents and school friends, but through one hour of captivating television over 13 Sunday nights, my perspective on the world exploded with curiosity and intrigue.

As well as all the stunning places David Attenborough travelled to, I was most absorbed by his amazing observations about animal behaviour, and his calm, soothing and engaging voice when he explained their behaviours so clearly. One of the most captivating episodes was with the mountain gorillas of Rwanda. While filming from a distance, the troop of gorillas came over to him and started playing with him and involving him in their family group. It was amazing footage, and it became abundantly clear how close humans are in evolutionary terms to our primate ancestors. (You can find this clip on YouTube – I suggest you do!) His observation was:

> There is more meaning and mutual understanding in exchanging a glance with a gorilla than with any other animal I know. Their sight, their hearing, their sense of smell is so similar to ours that they see the world in much the same way as we do. We live in the same sort of social groups with largely permanent family relationships. They walk around on the ground as we do, though they are immensely more powerful than we are. So if there were ever a possibility of escaping the human condition and living imaginatively in another creature's world, it must be with the gorilla. The male is an enormously powerful creature but he only uses his strength when he is protecting his family and it is very rare that there is violence within the group. So it seems really very unfair that man should have chosen the gorilla to symbolise everything that is aggressive and violent, when that is the one thing that the gorilla is not — and that we are.

From age 11 to the present day I have loved natural history documentaries, particularly by Sir David Attenborough … and I have realised I am an amateur anthropologist:

> **Anthropology:** the science of human beings; especially: the study of human beings and their ancestors through time and space and in relation to physical character, environmental and social relations, and culture.

I just have a natural love of observing how situations and interrelationships bring the best and worst out in people, and it is interesting to see how anthropology plays out in both life and the workplace.

As humans, we need to bear in mind we are still – in evolutionary terms – pretty new to the scene. Life started 3.8 billion years ago as single-cell organisms, and the fossil record shows that mammals have only been around for 200 million years, and Homo sapiens only for 200,000 years, or 0.004% of the time since life first appeared on Earth.

Understanding yourself

So why does any of this matter? It matters because we are still evolving and so are our behaviours. We are fundamentally social animals that operate in groups. Positive social interaction, love, caring, purpose and belonging are all fundamental human needs – we all need interaction, and they are at the heart of who we are. But also, more importantly, our interactions with others, both the positive and the negative, shape and define how we operate in the world, and are proven to be the most powerful determinant of our character, how we define our strengths, and how we define our morals or value system. These traits are at the very core of our Life Fingerprint.

From my own journey to define my best life, and help others to do the same, I have discovered that understanding what has defined and shaped 'Project Me' or my **Who** so far is crucially important. It defines our lens and perspective on the world, and our sense of self-worth. Once you do that study on yourself and go, *ahhh – that all makes sense, that is totally me!*, living the rest of your life by your own compass, versus what you think it *should* be, is completely and utterly liberating. Why? Because so many of us don't naturally feel great about ourselves. We all have insecurities and perceptions about ourselves and others that we let define us, rather than looking at ourselves as pure and simple 'Project Me', where we accept, I am what I am, and here's me … Once we do that and live with ourselves, Life Design becomes much more straightforward, and the fog about our path of what we really want from life lifts. We then start shaping our career, our leadership and our personal life in a way that is so totally and utterly us, and in a way that feels easy and effortless versus complex and a constant juggle.

So what does it take from you if you want to embark on the *Think. Plan. Live.* journey? It takes a preparedness to take a step back and look at your life, like an anthropologist would, as a set of behaviours and rituals that all have meaning. And once that is clear, to step back again to get perspective that will let you define who you are, what's important to you, and why you do what you do. Once that's clear, the future Life Design part all clicks into place with tremendous clarity, for your career, how you lead, and how you show up in your personal life. That approach will stand you in good stead to complete the **Who** section of the fingerprint, and also the subsequent **What, With, Why, Where** and **When**.

Discovering self-anthropology

So if I take this approach to myself, what early life clues were there that guided me on a 30-year corporate career path to a C-suite role at Coca-Cola, and then decide to change my path to one that helps others define their Life Fingerprint and live their best life? The interesting thing is the clues were there at an early age – I just didn't realise it at the time.

If I look at my own childhood, as I mentioned I grew up in Salisbury, a town with a population of only 40,000 people and a rich history as one of the earliest English settlements. The world heritage site of Stonehenge was only a few kilometres away. Living there I think sparked a strong sense of history that still lives on in me to this day.

If I project back to myself at school and my early years I was always naturally intelligent and curious, but not naturally confident. At age 11 I took what they call in the UK the 11+, which secured me a place at a selective girls' grammar school. In those early years I was a major frustration to my teachers. I was considered bright, but I found the style of teaching that expected you to memorise what you were taught in class and then just write it all verbatim again in tests really boring. I was naturally energetic, inquisitive and curious about the world, and had lots of questions about how stuff worked and why it was like that (remember … I saw myself as a mini David Attenborough), but my teachers were very 'old school' and I was seen as challenging, unwelcome and impertinent to ask all those annoying questions when I should just be copying stuff out of a textbook. As a result, I didn't feel confident and I didn't regard myself as being good at school work because I was unable to learn through memorising facts and figures – I only learned through doing, sensing and discussing. So I pretty much disengaged from school, and I would spend all my free time on sport. As a result, in my early high school years I would get my school work done but my reports weren't very impressive, commenting on what an energetic person I was but how that would be better deployed in the classroom versus on the sports field … but I didn't feel that way.

To the outside world I looked confident and undaunted about not being top of the class, but inside it really bothered me. I knew there were so many interesting ideas I wanted to share, discuss and explore about how the world worked … but no-one wanted to hear them.

At 15 my school life changed – six new teachers joined our school straight out of university. They were energetic and full of new ideas. They were less than a decade older than me, and their style of teaching really inspired me. One of them – Caroline Bateson – became my history teacher, and history became transformed from memorising dates and events to looking at the drivers and tipping points of historical changes. She saw a spark within me for new thoughts and ideas and really encouraged me to express my thoughts and perspectives. I was transformed from being a disengaged student to being enthusiastic and inspired. For the first time in my life I started to see how I thought and formed ideas, and my inquisitive and curious approach to life and problem solving became a real positive. She appeared interested and energised by my youthful enthusiasm and questioning versus the older teachers who relied on age and positional authority to keep me in line.

The biggest thing she did for me was build my confidence and build on my strengths, and as a result I believed in myself and what I could achieve. It was my first real learning that how we encourage and see other people in our lives has an incredible impact on how we make them think and feel about themselves. It showed me the power of seeing someone deeply enough so you could unlock their true potential, versus constraining and controlling them through authority.

From that point on I played to my passions and strengths. All the subjects I most enjoyed at school were centred around how the world worked: I chose geography, history and biology. I remember at the time I was told they didn't go together, and I was the only one in the school with that combination. But for me they made complete sense, because together they explained how Earth, nature and human relationships combined to create change. I had no idea why I liked that combination, until my revelation 30 years on that I am indeed 'built' to be an anthropologist and in fact have been one my whole life, as part of my Life Fingerprint, even if my career choice and path didn't have 'anthropology' in the title (funnily enough, not many in the business world do!). I have lived my life and led teams and organisations with anthropology and curiosity for human relationships at the heart of how I've performed those roles. And by sticking with subjects I truly enjoyed I rose from being an average student to winning the award for the best 'A' level results in the school. I know it would have been a very different story if I had done the expected thing of doing maths or languages. In hindsight, this was the first occasion for me, 35 years ago, that I realised that playing to your strengths while acknowledging your gaps was much more effective for achieving what you want in life, and that insight has proven to be true for me and every person I have coached in my life.

You may be wondering at this point why I have gone back 30-plus years to start the journey of Life Design. The reason is the clues of who I was had already been formed way back then. Observing who we are as children shows the best mirror of who we really are. A number of significant multi-year research studies have shown that our personalities stay pretty much the same throughout our lives, from our early childhood years to our old age, with personality traits observed in children being a strong predictor of adult behaviour.

> 'Give me a child until he is seven and I will show you the man.'
>
> **Aristotle**

So returning to my amazing teacher Caroline Bateson, her impact on me was transformational to the path I have followed in my life and career. I may have realised this to a small degree at the time, but – like most teenagers – I wasn't reflecting deeply on the meaning of life.

The lasting impact on my Life Fingerprint became clearer as life progressed. I have remained to this day someone passionate about seeing people for who they really are and bringing out the best in them. My own experience of feeling shut down and feeling undervalued means I never want to make anyone else feel the same way I did back at school. In fact, when I've experienced this sense of not being heard or where status or authority overrides collaboration and shared problem solving, I find the same feelings and emotions I felt at school coming to the surface again (it's one of my triggers!).

I have applied a strengths-based approach to myself and how I form and lead my teams and organisations. A core part of your Life Fingerprint is seeing who people really are, their true strengths and values, and unleashing them, and doing that with genuine interest and compassion. Contrast that approach with those people who act like a chameleon, adapting and changing to comply and keep others happy; my observation is if you do that there is only one guaranteed outcome: feeling undervalued and unfulfilled. So I highly recommend defining your Life Fingerprint versus being a chameleon.

FINDING MEANING IN THE RECURRING PATTERNS OF YOUR LIFE

My school experience is just one example of a pattern of behaviours that I have observed in myself and that I have observed in every client and friend I have navigated through Life Design. There are things we do, ways we react to stress, ways we learn, hobbies we enjoy, people and situations that inspire us that show up as patterns that repeat in our life. Observe these trends and discover these patterns and Life Design becomes much clearer. Go back to your Life Line exercise (starting on page 36) with that in mind and see what else you can discover looking at it again.

LIFE FINGERPRINT: WHO

So with the three exercises completed, pause to reflect on your **Who**, and complete the first part of your Life Fingerprint on the following page. Capture your values, strengths, and highs and lows.

WHO AM I?

Values (Top 5)

1. _____
2. _____
3. _____
4. _____
5. _____

Strengths (Top 5)

1. _____
2. _____
3. _____
4. _____
5. _____

My Highs are driven by (Key 5 Themes)

1. _____
2. _____
3. _____
4. _____
5. _____

My Lows are driven by (Key 5 Themes)

1. _____
2. _____
3. _____
4. _____
5. _____

Sparks and Jolts

Sparks and Jolts

Chapter 3

What do I like doing?

What you like doing in your career and personal life is the second key component of your Life Fingerprint. The **What** is often defined by your sources of inspiration and your interests and hobbies, guided by the values and strengths from your **Who**. I find the majority of people say it is hard to find time for what they like doing, so later in this chapter you will find some practical approaches to effectively managing your time, especially in your career.

PAYING ATTENTION TO INSPIRATION

Another clue to our patterns of what's important to us in life is what inspires us – those situations and people that really make us think and feel differently about ourselves or the world around us. To be yourself while paying attention to what inspires you is key. You can constantly collect inspiration in the same way you collect physical things.

I define inspiration in two main buckets – see if they work for you:

- **Sparks:** A Spark is a lightbulb or 'a-ha' moment. You can feel when this happens; someone says something or does something that makes you think or feel something. Pay attention to these sparks. It means that something or someone elicited a response in you. What they said or did triggered something. Responses can be positive or negative: 'I totally agreed with that – that's how I feel!' Or, 'That example is totally at odds with what I think – why?'

- **Jolts:** Jolts are more dramatic than Sparks. They are OMG moments, when you realise that something *big* just happened and you need to change or readjust something big in your life. It could relate to your job or career path, or a realisation that things need to change or move on in your personal life. Interestingly, I find significant life events or setbacks are people's biggest Jolts; for example, health problems, loss of someone you care about, a job that's going off the rails. Again, pay attention to your feelings and use the Jolt to trigger positive action rather than avoidance.

I've left pages for you to capture these moments as you read the book or in your everyday life. Start by capturing the triggers, then see what patterns appear.

Sparks should be happening to you regularly, Jolts every now and again. They can happen at any time, in more formal settings such as a meeting, conference or training, but also in everyday activities:

- 'A thought came to me while running … '

- 'I woke up in the middle of the night thinking about that … '

- 'That television program really made me think about … '

- 'My boss made me feel really good through what she said to me today … '

Typically Sparks and Jolts are triggered by what others say and do to us. These moments come and go, and what I have found is the tendency for most people is to ignore them. These little Sparks or bigger Jolts happen along with the other several thousand messages and stimuli we receive in our brains every day. We can't pay full attention to everything we read, hear and see, otherwise we would have sensory overload. But if you start watching out for them – 'that feeling' or 'that thought' – and start making a note when they occur, interesting patterns appear that give further clues to who you really are and your Life Fingerprint.

We all have the ability to create the kind of space we need for ourselves and others to show vulnerability and to provide the opportunity for a Spark or a Jolt, particularly if you – like me – are responsible for teams who look to you to model the right behaviour. (More on that in chapter 4.)

> 'Vulnerability is the birthplace of creativity, innovation and change.'
>
> **Brené Brown**

WHAT

Your sources of inspiration

When I first embarked upon Life Design I would ask people what their hobbies and interests were. Most people could rattle off a few, but then ended up concerned the list was a short one and so they would revert to a list of what they *used* to do:

- 'I used to play netball at university but not anymore.'

- 'When I was a student I loved to travel off the beaten track.'

- 'I used to paint.'

- 'I used to go to the cinema regularly.'

- 'I often used to go to galleries.'

You get the idea … our 'used to' list is often long, and each one of those things was important to us, but circumstances, time, career and children make them disappear into the past.

Hobbies and interests are things that excite, energise and inspire you, activities that you enjoy. What simple pleasures do you enjoy and give you energy and give you sparks of inspiration and enjoyment? You will have your own spring to mind. Some recent examples that people have shared with me are:

- 'With my best friend walking our dogs along the beach.'

- 'Playing football in the over 45s league.'

- 'Catching up with my rugby mates … even though we don't play anymore.'

- 'Bush walking in the national park with my family.'

- 'Watching a TED Talk.'

- 'By myself reading a book in a cafe with a view of the ocean.'

- 'Visiting museums and galleries.'

- 'Cooking Sunday lunch as a family.'

When people list what they enjoy they often regard these things as too simple or not counting as a hobby. But you know what: as long as you enjoy it, it gives you energy and you feel uplifted and inspired, that's all that counts! What really matters is that you actually find time to do some of the things on the list … So often, even if people can manage to get a good list together of things they enjoy, when I ask about when they last did something on the list there is often a long pause and a realisation that it wasn't recently. The next exercise should help you with your list.

My suggestion is to constantly seek out and find time for inspiration. As you can see from other people's examples, inspiration comes in many shapes and forms, and it is typically small and simple things that give us an uplift – focus less on collecting physical things and more on collecting inspiration.

FINDING AND DEFINING PATTERNS THROUGH SYNERGY

Patterns may already have started to emerge to you based on the exercises you have completed so far as part of discovering your **Who**. In the Synergy phase these insights combine **What** we like to do with **Who** and **Why**, to start to build a clearer picture of your Life Fingerprint.

Hobbies, interests and experiences

Below I have left a space for you to capture your hobbies, interests and favourite experiences for what inspires you. However small each one may seem or however big it feels, just write them all down, capturing the **What**, **With** and **Why** that drives your enjoyment and inspiration. When you have a full list, choose two of the simpler ones you will do in the next week. Start with a few simple, practical ones, then build up to the big ones.

WHAT

Another practical thing you can do is build a mood board of things that inspire you. There are lots of great free apps that let you do this. I do this on Pinterest and on Cluster.

What situations give you energy?

Now you have your inspiration list, think more about situations or experiences that give you energy. Examples from clients have included travelling to new places, playing golf with friends and swimming in the ocean. Some of these ideas may have come up in the last section. Here you can capture your thoughts on the ones that give you the most energy and capture them on the **What** Life Fingerprint page.

We will return more deeply to energy sources in the next chapter on **With** – for now, think more through the lens of the situation or activity that gives you energy.

What brings out the best in you at work?

The last part of inspiration gathering is reflecting on what brings the best out in you at work. What type of work do you enjoy doing? What is the work environment like? What is your boss like? How do you like to work? Again, capture your thoughts here and on the Life Fingerprint page.

Go with your intuition, blending current and old roles; maybe there were clues to this in your Life Line highs and lows that may trigger your thoughts.

(Later in this chapter we will explore how you can find time to integrate more of these things into your daily life.)

ARE YOU PRACTISING 3IS OR 3PS?

One of the best approaches to getting the most out of **What** you do is to really get stuck in. I chair a number of conferences and always open by asking delegates to live by the 3Is during the conference:

* Get *involved*.

* Get *immersed*.

* Get *inspired*.

Getting involved means asking questions, meeting new people, and really listening to the speakers or panellists.

Getting immersed means being deeply into it, submerged in the subject matter, to really take stuff in (only then do you get to experience the triggers of your Sparks and Jolts).

Getting inspired is an output of involvement and immersion. If you get involved and are immersed, inspiration follows (providing you chose your conference well in the first place!).

Asking people to sign up to this mantra completely changes the tone and engagement of what follows.

> 'Daring to set boundaries is about having the courage to love ourselves, even when we risk disappointing others.'
>
> **Brené Brown**

The next time you are at a conference, workshop or meeting, instead of just making lots of notes about what people say (trust me, you will never read them again – they will be 'filed' in your office, never to see the light of day again), make notes about Sparks, not just what was said but what it made you feel and what you want to do about it.

Try a simple test tomorrow – decide to go into the day with a mindset of being involved, being immersed and being inspired so you get the most out of situations, not just big things such as getting the most out of this two-day conference but also the little things, such as getting the most out of a meeting, conversation or phone call.

This may all seem obvious, but a remarkable number of people – dare I say it, the majority – instead adopt the 3Ps mindset: *passive, processing* and *perform.*

Passive is a bystander role – you look in on a situation or meeting and observe it, but you don't directly involve yourself. You may sit at the side seats in the room, take in your laptop and do your emails while in the meeting, observing but not speaking or asking questions.

Processing is when you look at and analyse a situation and compare it to your own mental model of how the world works. Processing is a comparative approach: *I will listen to what they say and compare it with what I think.* This is in contrast to immersing yourself and being open. Processors are still looking for meaning but it's comparative; they do ask questions, but comparing ones: 'How would that work versus what we do now?' Or they make statements like, 'We've tried that before and it didn't work.'

Perform is an 'impress me' mindset. Perform is subtle, and it brings to bear thoughts such as judging, where you rate the content and person speaking and decide whether they are up to the mark or not. Internal meetings, set up the wrong way without the right context, can run in this state; for example, the marketing team presenting to the sales team, or a new team presenting their business plan. This often turns into seeking to assert authority through questions or statements, rather than trying to explore and understand issues.

Practising the 3Is versus the 3Ps may sound simple, but don't knock it until you have tried it. Having looked into behavioural science studies, my approach is inspired by young children. Think about how young children view the world – with curiosity and intrigue as they try to work it all out. They are totally immersed, totally involved, and totally inspired. So get the most out of situations by being open minded, seeking to explore and understand through questioning rather than seeking to judge, classify and compartmentalise.

MANAGING YOUR CAPACITY, CAPABILITY AND PRODUCTIVITY

Another way to manage what you spend time on is to think about your work through three lenses, for yourself and – if you have a team – for each team member. I find it helps to think about what you do through the lenses of Capacity, Capability and Productivity, making a list of priorities in each:

- **Capacity:** Managing capacity is about how much time you have in your day and where you want to deploy it.

- **Capability:** This is being realistic about what your personal capabilities are. What do you find easy and effortless versus challenging and difficult? We should always be seeking to broaden our horizons and learn new things, but to be rewarding, what we spend time on should be a blend of core capabilities we already have and are confident in with learning a new capability or skill, which will take time.

- **Productivity:** The biggest enabler of spending the maximum amount of time on what you care about is being really strict at managing your own productivity. I can honestly say that people who own their personal productivity are the happiest and most effective at work.

I have elaborated below on some practical approaches to investing time in the right places. In so doing you will feel a great sense of control over what you spend your time on and how you cope with the stresses of managing conflicting priorities in what you are working on.

UNLOCKING MORE TIME

Many people feel that their options and the number of things they need to get done are constantly increasing, while the time available to do so is reducing ... how about you?

Do you feel like you're constantly juggling work and personal priorities? Are you feeling time stressed, with not enough hours in your busy working week to get it all done? If the answer is yes to both of these questions, you can reassure yourself that you are completely normal! I find that 9 out of 10 people I coach would agree.

But what about the 1 in 10 who feel they can find time for what's important to them; what practical tips and coping mechanisms can we learn from them? Let's find out ...

> 'We think, mistakenly, that success is the result of the amount of time we put in at work, instead of the quality of time we put in.'
>
> **Arianna Huffington**

How to find more time

I set myself the goal of finding and saving a whole day a week in the typical lives of busy senior leaders, so they could invest back into the things they really cared about and wanted to spend more time on. More time with the family; more 'me' time; more time for exercise; more time to rediscover old hobbies …

I am pleased to say I found the time, a life-changing 24 hours the typical person could save and reinvest. I've summarised the actions you can take to do this into simple steps you can test out for yourself. Some of you may find 24 hours, some less, but I guarantee if you give it a bit of thought you will unlock some time to reinvest in what you really care about.

Try it out and let me know if my TIME guide works for you.

<u>T</u>: Think and plan

Effective use of time is not an accident. Highly time-efficient people invest time thinking, planning and preparing. They put purpose behind how they manage their time. I have actually heard people say, 'I'm too busy to think' – this raises alarm bells, because without reflecting on where your time goes you have little chance of improving where you spend it.

> 'The best advice I could give anyone is to spend your time working on whatever you are passionate about in life.'
>
> **Richard Branson**

Think and plan by assessing the following issues.

Are you in a healthy 24-hour time regime? The ideal is 8 – 8 – 8 (eight hours each for sleep, work and personal life). Few manage the ideal, but how far are you away from that ideal? Too little sleep, too much work and too little time for your personal life is not good for your health. Work out which of the three you are neglecting so you can reinvest your time where it counts.

Great time planners set clear goals. Think through what you wished you had more time for. For many people it is reconnecting with some-thing you used to do. For example, some common complaints are:

- 'I have no time now to exercise.'

- 'I have to keep cancelling dinner with friends.'

- 'I haven't called my family overseas.'

- 'I haven't had a weekend away in a long time.'

Make a list and assess how much time you need to address such issues; for example, 'If I released five hours a week I would be able to go to the gym three times a week.' Once you have a goal, it will make saving the time to make that a reality more realistic, important and tangible.

Think about your 'only I can do this' list: these are the personal and business things that you and only you can do. It could be anything from reading a bedtime story to your kids each night to a critical team meeting you lead. The list should be short. If you have a very long list and the items on it fill most of your day, you need to have a rethink. You are likely not getting help from others or not delegating well at work.

In this 'Think and plan' phase, just think about these areas – we will come back to the list later.

I: Invest work time wisely

Most of my clients have successful careers, teams to manage, and busi-ness commitments and goals they want to achieve. The challenge is how to be a successful leader without spending all your waking hours work-ing. The answer lies in how you invest your time. Let's have a look at some common issues:

- **ROIT:** In business we talk a lot about ROIC (return on invested capital) as a key metric; I want to start a movement towards ROIT (return on invested time). Successful time managers think of time as a valuable asset that they invest. They 'invest' time versus 'spend' time. One of the most positive investments they typically make is in developing and coaching their teams, because this in turn frees up more of their time to 'lead' versus 'do'.

- **Reshape your meetings:** The largest time saver for most people is in reshaping their working day. Successful time savers focus their work time around what's most important and urgent, they decide which meetings they attend, and formulate their working day for maximum productivity. For most people the biggest time saving in the 24 hours saved is in cutting back on meetings that waste time; on average two hours of the working day is spent in wasted meetings. That's 10 hours a week!

  Many of the meetings you attend are scheduled by other people; these are the first place to look for time. If you find yourself leaving meetings saying 'that was a complete waste of time', you need to make a change! Remember, you often have a choice. Just because you are invited, you don't always have to attend. You can go to the most relevant part, or you can say no if it's not adding value. Getting out of wasteful meetings will give you back not only time but also energy.

  You also need to own and shape the meetings you run. Highly effective teams set clear agendas; reading is sent in advance and outcomes and goals are clear. I found that the more effective the leader of the meeting was, the shorter the meeting. Think about your monthly all-day meetings or half-day weekly meetings and take ownership of reshaping them to release time not just for you but also for your team.

- **Save time on the commute:** The savings here can easily be a 30-minute saving a day. One way to save this time is avoiding driving in peak-hour traffic; it's both frustrating and it wastes time. I know people who work from home catching up on emails first thing and head into the office after the rush. And even more time could be saved by working from home some days. Most companies allow some flexibility: successful time managers use this, unsuccessful ones don't.

These simple changes can save you many hours in a week. Have a careful look at your schedule and lifestyle to see where else you can save some time.

> 'The difference between successful people and
> really successful people is that really successful
> people say no to almost everything.'
>
> **Warren Buffett**

_M_: Make and manage choices

Everyone has only 24 hours in a day. Time is finite, so making choices and managing that time wisely makes a big difference. Let's see how you can do this:

- **Stick to your priorities:** If you successfully thought about and planned your time in the 'think and plan' step above, this step is all about keeping on track. Highly effective time planners stick close to their plan. Of course there is flexibility and things will shift, but your goal is to stay on track.

- **Openly share your commitments, and encourage others to do the same:** This is a proven method to stay on track; for example, telling your colleagues you play tennis on a Monday evening will avoid people scheduling late meetings that day. Trust me, it works. Most people you work with don't get up in the morning trying to mess up your time plan, but if they don't know about your plans then they could. Scheduling time for personal commitments in the evening also helps you leave the office: dinner with the family; sport; the latest film with friends. Many people find that in not planning their personal life, their work life fills the time. If you have a goal to leave at 6 pm, just do it, otherwise you may still be there working at 10 pm. There is _always_ more work to do.

_E_: Eliminate and delegate

So by now we have recovered some time from meetings, commuting and better managing time, but there is still more time to be found by eliminating some activities and delegating to others. Let's have a look:

- **Eliminate the lost time and win it back:** On closer review, most people find they have a lot of time tied up in activities not on their priority list. Time spent on social media, games and apps could be reinvested with humans! Most people can find 30 minutes on average a day from these activities, giving you 3.5 hours a week.

Another time waster is 'always on' television. Watching just a program you really like rather than carrying on to watch the one that follows saves you at least an hour each time. Add 1.5 hours of background television that you can drop to your social media savings and you are up to 5 hours saved.

- **Delegate to others:** This is where the 'only I can do this' list from your thinking and planning time should be reviewed. Release time by focusing only on the important things on your list – delegate the rest. At home this could include outsourcing household tasks such as cleaning, gardening or getting the groceries delivered. Your goal is to find at least one thing you can offload. It could also involve enlisting your kids to help out more. Savings from this should be at least 3 hours a week.

    At work, if you have invested time in your people you should ideally be surrounded by a capable team who you can delegate to and make feel empowered. This releases time for your 'only I can do this' list, and results in a happier and more motivated team who can get the job done. The minimum saving is usually about 3 hours, and over the long run it can be much, much more.

So that's the TIME guide! In this example 24 hours – or one day – a week was saved (10 hours from wasted meetings, 3 hours of commute time, 3.5 hours from wasted time on social media, 1.5 hours of television, 3 hours from delegating or outsourcing household tasks, and 3 hours team delegation at work). Your savings will I am sure be different, but with a bit of focus on your return on invested time you can, I'm sure, unlock some valuable time to reinvest into something else you care about.

> 'Imagine life as a game in which you are juggling some five balls in the air. You name them – work, family, health, friends and spirit – and you're keeping all of these in the air. You will soon understand that work is a rubber ball. If you drop it, it will bounce back. But the other four balls – family, health, friends and spirit – are made of glass. If you drop one of these, they will be irrevocably scuffed, marked, nicked, damaged or even shattered. They will never be the same. You must understand that and strive for balance in your life.'
>
> **Brian Dyson, Former CEO Coca-Cola Enterprises**

Have you got a wonky Life Wheel? Life has trade offs and choices, and for many people it feels like you have to be an expert at spinning plates to keep everything on track. Looking at your life through the lens of a wheel to see if it's balanced or wonky can shed some light on what to focus and prioritise.

There are a few major areas that make up the core part of everyone's life and they can be clustered and summarised into eight categories:

- **career and work:** work hours, career direction, purpose/meaning, performance

- **financial security and money:** budgeting, saving, income, investment

- **health and wellbeing:** eating habits/diet, fitness, sleep, relaxation, emotional health, self-care

- **family and friends:** relationships, time, quality, support, community

- **relationships and romance:** partner, communication, intimacy, space

- **personal growth:** education, learning, reading, awareness, connecting, spirituality

- **fun and recreation:** leisure, hobbies, passion, laughter

- **physical environment:** home, location, appearance, transport.

As you reflect on your Life Wheel it's a good opportunity for you to map what's right for you and your current priorities and then map them to be your future end state. There are no right and wrong answers or priorities; it should reflect *your* reality. I acknowledge that for some people they feel constrained in some shape or form in their life – financially maybe, or through health – and an aspect of the wheel can trigger that you are constrained in some way. Looking at your Life Wheel is not done in some idealist vacuum, it is done with a good dose of practicality and realism – so please bring that to bear in the upcoming exercise.

But the cautionary note on this is to catch yourself if you start to feel powerless to change or a victim to an aspect of your Life Wheel. Think instead what you could change if you made the choice to, and ask the question, 'What would it take?'

SYNERGY: LIFE WHEEL EXERCISE

All aspects of the Life Wheel are important to us to feel we are in balance, but the relative importance and emphasis differs from person to person. This simple exercise of mapping out your Life Wheel and giving each life area a 1 to 10 score for how you are tracking on that aspect of your life will often bring up a few realities – some scores may be lower than you expect and want, and some will be okay. If the life wheel truly was a wheel, it would often be pretty wonky and need a few adjustments to run smoothly.

YOUR LIFE WHEEL

- Complete this exercise for yourself in the following pages. Firstly, assess your current reality 1 to 10 for each aspect of the wheel, and then repeat the exercise again for what your future ideal wheel would look like. For each gap in your scores, capture a few areas that would improve the score from the current level to the desired level.

- Reflect on any Sparks and Jolts as you complete this exercise and make a note of them; we will return to these thoughts in the integration phase of Life Design in our chapter on **When**.

Current Life Wheel

The eight sections of the wheel represent your current life balance. If you view the centre of the wheel as 0 and the outer edge as 10, rank your level of satisfaction with each life area by drawing a line to create a new outer edge (see example below).

Example

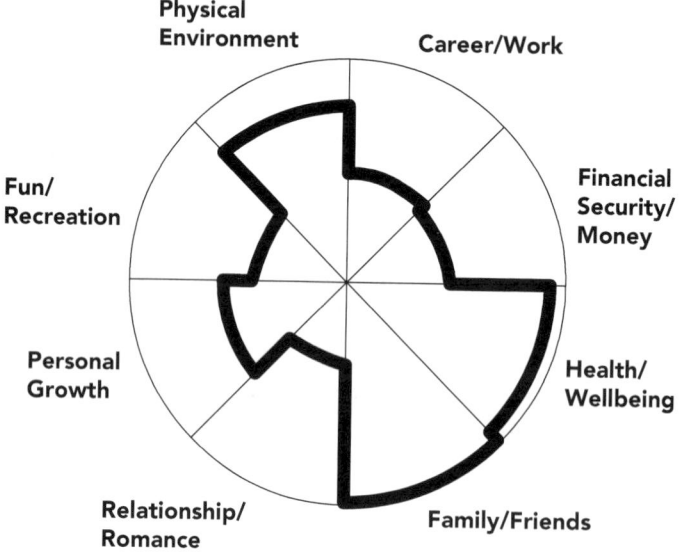

LIFE WHEEL

Current Life Wheel

Physical Environment
Home
Location
Appearance
Transport

Career/Work
Work hours
Career direction
Purpose/meaning
Performance

Financial Security/ Money
Budgeting
Saving
Income
Investment

Fun/ Recreation
Leisure
Hobbies
Passions
Laughter

Personal Growth
Education
Learning
Reading
Awareness
Connecting
Spirituality

Health/ Wellbeing
Eating habits/diet
Sleep
Relaxation
Emotional health
Self care

Relationship/ Romance
Partner
Communication
Intimacy
Space

Family/ Friends
Relationships
Time
Quality
Support
Community

Future Life Wheel

Capture in your wheel opposite what your ideal would look like 1 to 10 for each aspect of your wheel. And I've left some room below for you to make some notes.

LIFE WHEEL

Future Life Wheel

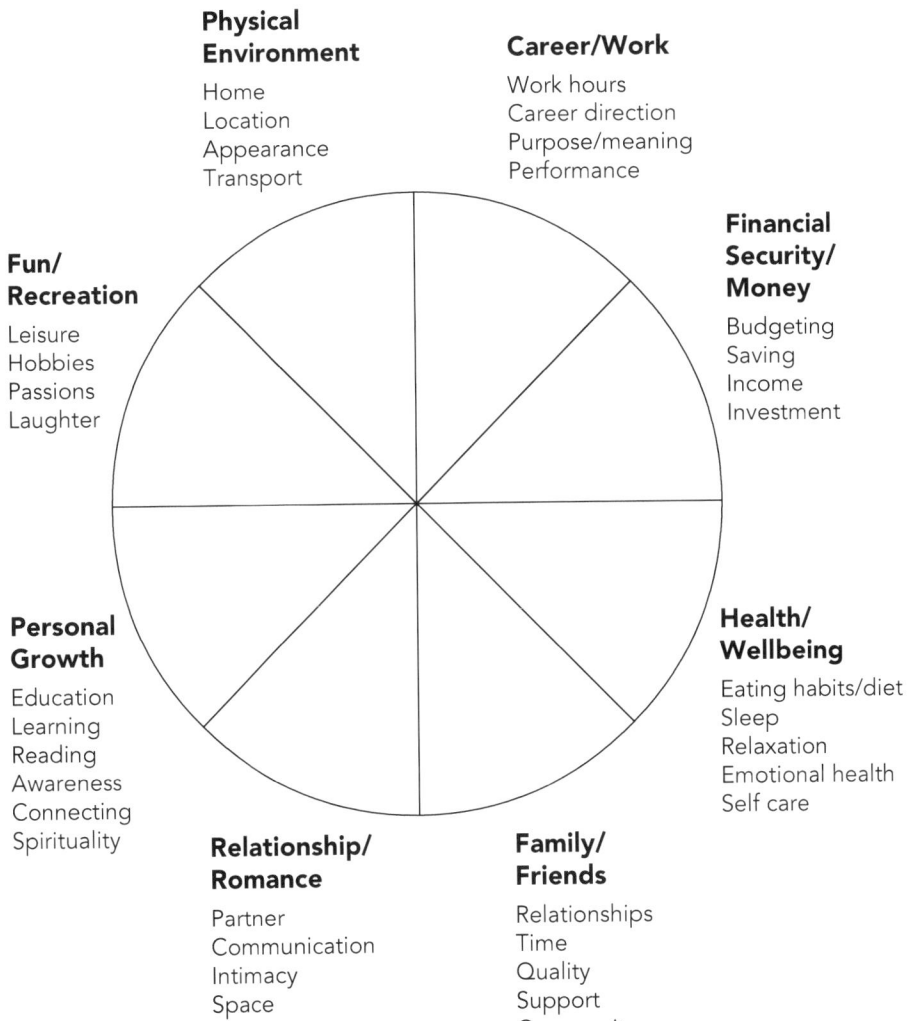

Physical Environment
Home
Location
Appearance
Transport

Career/Work
Work hours
Career direction
Purpose/meaning
Performance

Financial Security/ Money
Budgeting
Saving
Income
Investment

Fun/ Recreation
Leisure
Hobbies
Passions
Laughter

Personal Growth
Education
Learning
Reading
Awareness
Connecting
Spirituality

Health/ Wellbeing
Eating habits/diet
Sleep
Relaxation
Emotional health
Self care

Relationship/ Romance
Partner
Communication
Intimacy
Space

Family/ Friends
Relationships
Time
Quality
Support
Community

Observations from your Life Wheel

Life category	Wheel observations (current)	Current rating
Career and work		
Financial security and money		
Health and wellbeing		
Family and friends		
Relationship and romance		
Personal growth		
Fun and recreation		
Physical environment		

Desired future end state, what needs to change?	Future rating	Priority rank 1–8 each life category

The Life Wheel alongside the Life Line form the core 'life check' parts of Life Design. As you planned your desired future state you would no doubt have found some things are 100% within your control, some things you will want to achieve with others, and there will be some things where you may feel you need greater help.

> 'Wealth is the ability to fully experience life.'
> **Henry David Thoreau**

On the page following you may find it helpful to capture the follow-up actions for your biggest change priorities for your Life Wheel. Some examples from other people have been provided below to get you going ...

Actions I can take	Actions with others	Where I need help
Go to the gym	Planning our next family holiday together	I need a better financial plan; I need a financial adviser
Eat more healthily	Reintroduce family Sunday lunch	I need to go to see the doctor about ...
Regain my 'me time'	Book a regular 'date night' with my partner	I need to go to see the physio about my back
Visit a gallery or museum	Talk to my boss about my career and development	
Restart painting	Book a night out with my best friends	

Life Wheel follow-up actions

Actions I can take	Actions with others	Where I need help

WHAT

LIFE FINGERPRINT: WHAT

So with the inspiration-gathering exercise completed through the lenses of interests and hobbies, experiences, energy situations, and ideal work, pause to reflect on your **What**, and complete the second part of your Life Fingerprint.

WHAT
do I enjoy doing?

My interests and hobbies... (Top 5)

1. _____
2. _____
3. _____
4. _____
5. _____

My favourite experiences are... (Top 5)

1. _____
2. _____
3. _____
4. _____
5. _____

My energy giving situations are... (Top 5)

1. _____
2. _____
3. _____
4. _____
5. _____

At work I am at my best when I am...

1. _____
2. _____
3. _____
4. _____
5. _____

Sparks and Jolts

Chapter 4

<u>With</u> ... Who do I like doing things with?

It was important to first fully reflect on **Who** we are and **What** we like doing, ahead of focusing on **With**, because the clarity that comes from knowing ourselves guides us on which people in our lives are going to bring out the best and worst in us and others. Innumerable studies have shown that long-term happiness is most clearly defined by human connection with others. At the core of human happiness is *belonging* ... to feel you belong, to love and be loved ... to feel you can show up with others and be you ... 100% you – that is a universal truth. A 75-year-long Harvard study showed that this was the biggest predictor of a long and happy life.

Another interesting observation is that we are the average of the five people we spend the most time with. Who we spend time **With** – family, friends and colleagues – has an incredible impact on our Life Fingerprint. In this chapter we will explore both how we observe or judge others and also which people are our Energy Givers, Sloths and Vampires.

We will also explore the importance of leadership and team effectiveness as a deeper dive on how the **With** part of the Life Fingerprint impacts on leadership and team effectiveness.

THE POWER OF CURIOSITY AND CONNECTION

> 'If you want to go fast, go alone. If you
> want to go far, go together.'
>
> **African proverb**

It is in our human nature to judge people – call it measuring up, or just simply those thoughts that pop into our head ... *I don't know why they did or said that; I don't know what they were thinking when they decided to wear that* ... Our brain is constantly triggering these thoughts. But if they are not kept in check, we may find we are living a 'comparative' life versus a 'live and let live' life.

If we judge others, or if they perceive we are judging them, they feel it. I don't know about you, but I know I don't like it when people jump to conclusions or express their opinion on something about me without really knowing where I am coming from. I also find for my coaching clients, one of the biggest derailers people face to their self-esteem is the sense of feeling judged by other people – their bosses, peers, friends, partners, kids ...

This quote sums it up for me:

> 'Before you judge my life, my past, or my character
> ... Walk in my shoes, walk the path I have travelled,
> live my sorrow, my doubts, my fear, my pain and my
> laughter. Remember, everything has a story. When
> you have lived my life then you can judge me.'
>
> **Unknown (but a wise person)**

So what can you do about this? It's good to practise a practical alternative to how you build connections with others, rather than making judgements. You can also turn that same approach around when you feel judged, to really understand what is going on behind the scenes.

1. Connect and context first

The better we understand and build rapport and relate to each other, the stronger our connections become. By putting ourselves in other people's shoes, we begin to feel what they feel, not just think what they think. And they'll start responding the same way.

Context is important too; what situation are they in to make them come across that way? How's their day been? What's happening in their world right now?

2. Seek to understand

If we automatically try to judge what others are saying and doing, we can't understand them. We might accurately assume they're wrong or right, but we won't know *why* they chose that path. So suspend judgement and seek to *understand* before seeking to be *understood*. You can do that practically by asking open questions rather than jumping to conclusions.

3. Try curiosity instead

The less you judge others, the more receptive they'll be to what you say and do.

I've found that by replacing judgement with curiosity and interest I'm able to get a better handle on what's going on, and as a result be more perceptive. If a topic or situation is a tricky one to ask questions about, such as someone getting angry in a meeting or someone overreacting on email, try to think about what is going on in their world. *Why would they be doing or saying that? What values or perspective are they coming from? What would motivate them? What are they feeling?*

> 'If you don't like something, change it. If you can't change it, change your attitude.'
>
> **Maya Angelou**

Typically – and if you think about it, unsurprisingly – situations, decisions and reactions are triggered by who we are, our values and our strengths – basically our take on life. This gives us different perspectives, which in turn impact our motivations and how we show up in life.

So don't think in terms of good and bad at first. Instead, think in terms of motivation: why does this person think or act this way? In my own case it is a kind of anthropology; my view is that people (or at least most people) are inherently good. We all have our own complex version of life going on and a whole load of things we are dealing with, so better to be curious and understand what's behind the behaviour versus judging how it shows up. Live and let live.

DEFINING YOUR ENERGY GIVERS, SLOTHS AND VAMPIRES

> 'I define connection as the energy that exists between people when they feel seen, heard, and valued; when they can give, and receive without judgment; and when they derive sustenance and strength from the relationship.'
>
> **Brené Brown**

We all have people and situations that give us energy or take energy away. Energy is the source of action, positive or negative, so it's important to understand the sources of energy for us so we can keep ourselves topped up with positive energy and avoid situations or people that zap our energy.

Imagine there are three types of energy sources or energy drains:

- **Energy Givers:** These are people who when you are with them you feel a spark of enthusiasm and inspiration and you know you do more exciting things, think more and learn more in their company.

  What are the places and activities that give you energy? Is it a walk near the ocean? Walking in a forest? Watching a TED Talk, or the buzz of the city? Physical spaces and environments have a big impact on our energy.

- **Energy Sloths:** These are people who when you are with them you gossip more or don't do anything new. It's okay to be around these people, but don't do it for too long or you will feel your energy slowly ebbing away.

Places that can be sloth-like could be being in front of the television or social media for too long.

- **Energy Vampires:** These are people who when you are with them you feel your energy being drained because they are negative and 'glass half empty'. They tend to dwell on negatives. They tend to talk about themselves. At work it could be a boss or colleague with endless requests but giving no thanks ...

    Places and activities that are Vampires can be a job that you don't like or tasks you hate doing. The answer here is to have a rethink, or if it's a task outsource it to someone it gives energy to.

> 'No-one can make you feel inferior without your consent.'
>
> **Eleanor Roosevelt**

WITH

Notes

SYNERGY: DEFINING YOUR SOURCES OF ENERGY EXERCISE

So if you like the idea of defining and managing your energy levels, complete this energy sources exercise for yourself.

YOUR SOURCES OF ENERGY

Use the table on pages 124–125 to make a list of the people and situations that are your Energy Givers, Energy Sloths and Energy Vampires. Hopefully some Sparks will come through from your list. What people or places give you energy? Are you finding enough time for them? Who or what are your energy zappers? How do you reduce time spent with these people or on these activities so you can release that time back to the Energy Givers? These lists I guarantee will be enlightening and, at times, scary. Your goal should be to minimise your time with the vampires and maximise your time with the givers, so capture your 'a-ha' moments in the exercise and any other Sparks and Jolts that come to mind. I've provided some examples in the first table.

WITH

Sources of energy example

Mode/Action	Energy Giver
Typical characteristics	• Enthusiastic • Smiles and engages all around them • Encourages • Helps you think • Makes you feel good • Gives you honest feedback • Looks to help you • Sparks thoughts or ideas in you • Takes the initiative
List current people in your life that have that effect on you (at work and in your personal life)	Add real people's names here … be honest with yourself. Sometimes it is a person plus a situation rather than all the time; if so capture that.
List current situations that put you in that energy mode yourself	Tips/Examples • When I am doing X • When I am with X
List situations, inspiration, desperation, people that put you in that energy mode yourself	Tips/Examples • Walking on the beach • Watching a TED Talk • Out for dinner with … • On holiday with the family

Energy Sloth	Energy Vampire
• Smiles at friends • Consistent • Not into trying new things • Doesn't take the initiative • Gossips about others • Waits for tasks • Does what is required; does just what is asked	• Doesn't smile much • Negative, glass half full • Critical • Blames • Reacts to work • Does less than is needed, need to chase them • Expecting but thankful
Tips/Examples • When I feel unappreciated	Tips/Examples • When I face stress at work

Make a list of the people and situations that are your Energy Givers, Energy Sloths and Energy Vampires, and complete the table.

Mode/Action	Energy Giver
Typical characteristics	
List current people in your life that have that effect on you (at work and in your personal life)	
List current situations that put you in that energy mode yourself	
List situations, inspiration, desperation, people that put you in that energy mode yourself	

Energy Sloth	Energy Vampire

How did you find the energy exercise?

> 'I've learned that people will forget what you said, people will forget what you did, but people will never forget how you made them feel.'
>
> **Maya Angelou**

I observe very different reactions to the energy exercise. Even though the exercise is about exploring who drives those energy levels in us, many people focus on themselves and get a wake-up call – either good or bad – about how they show up to others. If you have become stuck and think you are an Energy Vampire, may I suggest you focus harder on the energy-giving side of the equation and really work that through.

The goal for the energy exercise is that you become aware of where your energy is coming from, and that you minimise time with the Vampires and maximise time with the Energy Givers. If you think of your energy levels like a personal battery, the goal is that you stay fully charged up, because with energy in place we can face most things the world throws at us. If you allow your energy to get low, any small setback can take you into an energy deficit. This simple tool is therefore an enabler of pro-actively managing not only your energy but also your stress levels.

Keep in your head the idea of balancing your energy sources and stay topped up as a battery, so you are running nearer 100% rather than running on empty.

WHAT ABOUT IQ AND EQ IN BUILDING YOUR CAREER?

Assuming competence is in place, you achieve things at work when the teams you are in or lead work effectively, and at the core of that is show-ing up and utilising your full EQ (emotional intelligence) versus relying on your IQ.

Despite this, I still see many people seeking to build their career through IQ and not demonstrating EQ. They put all their energy into building their competency rather than building their connections. Com-petency is a prerequisite for success – you have to be good at what you do. But increasingly I see the differentiator in career progression is con-nection with others (EQ) versus competency (IQ).

> 'Look for three things in a person: intelligence,
> energy and integrity. If they don't have the last
> one, don't even bother with the first two.'
>
> **Warren Buffett**

Great leadership takes a good level of IQ, blended with a very high level of common sense, combined with high EQ.

Our intelligence level we are basically born with. Of course we build knowledge and understanding of the world over time, but our underlying level of IQ is pretty stable. It's part of our **Who**. Where we can really grow our intelligence is in the area of emotional intelligence, and in the area of leadership it has now been proven that EQ is a much better determinant of leadership success than IQ. Academic intelligence may have got us in the door when we were graduates, but career progression – particularly to senior leadership – is all about EQ, and this defines how well we work **With** others.

There are many models of EQ. The simplest one, which I prefer to use, revolves around five main areas:

- **Self-awareness:** knowing what you are feeling, when you are feeling it.

- **Self-regulation:** using your emotions to serve you and not get in your way.

- **Motivation:** being goal oriented and having a positive attitude.

- **Empathy:** sensing what other people are feeling, and seeking other perspectives.

- **Social skills:** the ability to comfortably interact and cooperate with others.

Managing these five aspects of EQ in balance is the key to managing relationships with others.

THE POWER OF BEING INCLUSIVE

At the core of successfully navigating the workplace, life and ultimately to be a great leader, how we engage, inspire and collaborate with other people is proven to be the biggest determinant of success. A proven way to stretch our thinking and horizons is to surround ourselves, particularly at work, with different types of people who look, think and act differently to you. Forming a network and team that is inclusive of new thinking and perspectives has been proven to unlock greater progress and breakthroughs in thinking, doing and innovation. A good start is just showing up in life that way, by getting to understand people first instead of judging them or jumping to conclusions about them before getting to know them. You may be reading this thinking *that's okay, I already do that*, but let's look once more into our brains and see how it actually works.

Escaping your own biases

Our brain has assimilated and processed millions of situations, bits of information and thoughts over several decades of stimulus, and that data is stored in our brain as memory as thoughts and feelings. To help us quickly process new information, the brain classifies new data based on this stored information. When faced with new situations, we make rapid conclusions based upon what we already know and have experienced. This rapid decision making is unconscious; the brain calls on all those decades of stored thoughts to make a quick decision in micro seconds.

Visualise your brain with a one-metre ruler as a measuring stick alongside it. There are lines on the stick marked out for experiences stored in your brain: your parents' opinions and actions, your schools and teachers, your friends' outlook on life, your home town and who lived there, your travel experiences, your work and your colleagues, what you have read, what you have watched, politicians' opinions, your experiences of war or terrorism, your experiences of pain or loss … it goes on and on. The list of stored experiences that make up your one-metre ruler are unique to you, and – like it or not – those experiences show up in your decision making about people and situations.

This is why first impressions count and we create a view on someone in the first few seconds. But this fast brain wiring is also responsible for creating bias in how we process new stimuli, because without decision making being conscious and instead being unconscious we rely on past experiences and norms to come to conclusions versus assessing real facts. This is all crucially important because this plays out in how we assess and judge people; even if rationally we don't think we are, we can't help ourselves – 'it's our brain's fault'.

> 'Humility is not thinking less of yourself,
> it's thinking of yourself less.'
>
> **C.S. Lewis**

That makes complete sense, right? That we would be shaped by the world around us, and that this forms our measuring stick against which any new experience is judged? How this expresses itself is we classify things using our take on the world. Take, for example, something that I find bizarre – that we classify whole generations based on another generation's lens on the world. Let's take a typical example: baby boomers and millennials. To baby boomers, millennials are 'high maintenance', don't respect seniority, don't dress appropriately for work, and want too much freedom in how and where they work. To millennials, baby boomers are too hung up on age and seniority, dress in an overly formal way, are set in their ways, like routines and structured ways of working, and seem more focused on how you work than output.

Of course you will be reading this thinking your rational brain is working, and perhaps you think it is strange to classify and generalise about a generation in these ways. But experiments have shown we 'process' and judge people through the lens of unconscious decision making all the time (even if we don't mean to), and it plays out in how we show up as a leader and create teams too.

Studies have been conducted where the same CV was sent to recruiters and all that was changed was the name. One study found that feedback on the candidates fundamentally shifted depending on what the recruiter thought the gender and race of the applicant was. This included recruitment fundamentals such as how they assessed their qualifications, experience and expertise, and the capability to do the advertised role.

Now if you had asked the recruiter whether they thought bias was at play they would adamantly deny it was, but the results showed that unconsciously these thoughts were at play in decision making. You only need to look at the gender- and race-related construct of major companies to know that this isn't just showing up in research, it is fully alive and kicking in the workplace.

Recognition of bias in recruiting resulted late in 2016 with the Australian Public Sector Commission starting a recruitment trial to use 'blind CVs' in the hope the process would create a more diverse hiring pool from which the best applicants could be selected. Names, birth dates,

WITH

gender and postcodes of applicants for public service positions were cut from applications and CVs in a trial aimed at removing bias in hiring, and this process is used to conduct first-cut shortlists for roles. Later in the process, information such as the applicant's age, gender, ethnic background or socioeconomic status is revealed.

So what?

So what is the 'so what' in all of this? I want you to reflect on how this shows up for you in how you construct and lead project teams. It is 100% guaranteed we all have biases in some shape or form. If our brain has to process 70,000 pieces of information a day it has no choice but to process information through shortcuts, and that includes shortcuts we have learned about society, gender, age, culture and religion. The only thing you can do about it is shift your thoughts from the limbic or emotional part of your brain where the shortcuts exist and move them into the neocortex, where you really think about what your biases are. That way you will start to realise your biases and can start to pay attention to them. If you are interested in going deeper there are free tests online. The most comprehensive is the Implicit Association Test created by Harvard University.

* * *

Test or no test, the action here is to pay more attention to who you spend time with, and ask yourself, 'Do they all look and behave like me, or are they diverse in backgrounds, culture, gender, age and perspective … ?'

GETTING HELP AND SUPPORT TO BUILD YOUR CAREER

Mentorship and sponsorship

In building my career, what I have found is for sure you need to be capable and competent at what you do. But this is only part of the jigsaw, and interestingly as you get more senior, not the most important part. How you connect, communicate and collaborate with your boss, your boss's boss, your peers and your team will be a far greater determinant of how far you will progress up the career ladder than pure job competency.

Business pure and simple is about relationships; people like to work with people they know, respect, feel are authentic and whom they trust. That is human nature. I have held that principle true for the whole of my working life, and anyone I observe following this philosophy, I've found it works for them too.

But this section is about mentoring and sponsorship ... so why have I started with relationships? The answer is that mentors and sponsors are people you build rapport and a connection with. For me, building relationships with bosses, peers and teams is crucial for me to enjoy my job. If I don't, I don't feel a big enough sense of belonging, and that is needed so I know the people around me have my back when I need them, and of course I have theirs.

There is a lot of coverage on the importance of having mentors and sponsors, particularly in relation to the progress of women into senior positions. It's in press articles, books, and a live topic at many a conference and workshop. Having been a panellist at several women-in-leadership conferences and courses that went deeper on the topic, my simple observation is that mentorship and sponsorship need to be demystified, because to most women in the room their perception of what was needed to get mentors and sponsors was to go to big networking events, or ask senior leaders they didn't know to mentor them, or to wait in line for their company to set up an official mentoring or sponsorship program in which, if they were 'lucky', they would be asked to participate in.

> 'Train people well enough so they can leave, treat them well enough so they don't want to.'
>
> **Richard Branson**

What I can share from my own experience, and what was a common thread across all the senior leaders I shared the stage with on panels discussing this topic, is firstly we didn't call it mentoring or sponsorship, we just called it collaboration or relationship building and we saw the relationships we built at work as reciprocal. We gained a benefit from working closely with other people, and so did they; it was a two-way street. So I recommend that you give advice if asked as well as receiving it. Giving advice to mentors builds mutual trust.

WITH

Another consideration when developing mentors is consciously reflecting and communicating what you would like to learn from them. The skill of a great mentor is to bring out the best in you and help you develop professionally. Also seek to include people who are different to you, to stretch your thinking. In my experience, the most rewarding mentor–mentee relationships are built on mutual interest and respect. As a mentee it is most effective to approach someone you know or work with who already inspires you in a specific area, such as with their leadership style, their entrepreneurial skills or how they engage and inspire their team. Choosing a core focus area you are working on gives the mentor specific insight on how they can help you. This forms the basis of a strong mutual relationship. From a mentoring perspective, great mentors receive many requests from potential mentees, so make sure you stand out. Most mentors enjoy mentoring people who are eager to learn and apply that inspiration to achieve more in their career. Mentors get a buzz out of seeing their mentees achieve, so if you are a great mentee you will attract the right mentors.

A crucial part of the mentor–mentee relationship is being open to feedback and advice. As a mentee you should be open to asking for opinions, perspectives, and 'how to' do something. Your mentor should also ask you lots of good, open, probing questions to help you learn to problem solve. I find it interesting that despite this being a core part of mentoring, what sets apart the mentees that make the most progress is being completely open and non-defensive about feedback. They hear feedback, clarify it, absorb it and do something about it.

If you build your career while building relationships you will build mentors too, and if you keep in contact, these relationships can stay in place for the long term. You will find along the journey some of those mentors may rate what you do so highly that they will recommend you to others. If they do, they become a sponsor.

There are more complex models out there on securing mentors and sponsors, but try this approach – it will take the pressure off you …

BRINGING THE POWER OF <u>WITH</u> TO LEADERSHIP

Leadership sits across all 6Ws of the Life Fingerprint, however we will go deeper on it in this **With** section of the Fingerprint, because the biggest determinant of leadership success (assuming core competency is already in place) is how effectively you work with other leaders, peers and your team. Leadership is a journey, and like any other aspect of your career you learn lessons along the way.

Are you a leader or a manager?

My reflections on my own leadership journey and what I have seen in other leaders is an evolution of leadership. For most leaders, the journey starts with being appointed to be a manager of other people. Most people get to that position by being great at their job rather than for their leadership potential.

Just because you are appointed a manager doesn't mean you are a leader. I see too many people act only as managers. They use their position to get results, with the team simply being told what to do rather than being involved in a collaborative process. People who manage versus lead are characterised by a heavy task focus, handing tasks to the team and getting back output. This relationship is a transactional one between the manager and the team, and if you asked these team members they would be unmotivated to do any more than just complete the required tasks.

What characterises the shift from manager to leader is building a connection and relationship with each member of your team, through understanding where they are at, their strengths, their goals and their aspirations. The foundation of any leadership is team connection and mutual understanding. Once you know your team, you are able to harness their skills and bring out the best in them to get great results. They will start to respect you as a leader rather than see you as a manager. Respect is built through leading by example. This mutual respect between a leader being authentic and open and the team showing up and being able to do the same creates mutual value and respect. It is the breeding ground of open, honest dialogue, a results focus and ultimately momentum, because the team is all pulling in the same direction, not because they are compelled to through management but because they want to.

Leadership at its best is highly adaptive – adaptive to the changing external business environment and also highly adaptive to a team's needs. Leadership is also highly situational. If you accept that every team member is different then you must lead and develop them to get the best out of their strengths. This adaptive approach ensures each team member feels personally valued and developed.

WITH

Build a reputation as a great leader and people will want to work for you. Great leaders attract aspiring great leaders.

Building great teams

Another skill in more advanced leadership is to be able to form teams based on the business challenges you face. Good leaders can attract other good leaders who are like them. Great leaders seek out a greater diversity of skills or perspectives to complement and complete their own skill set. They also seek out others who they think can be even better leaders than they are. They are great at spotting potential. They are open with their team about their leadership strengths and gaps, and that openness breeds team openness too, so everyone can operate at their best by using their strengths. I am a big believer in strengths-based leadership. Lead through your strengths and your passion and commitment come through all the more. Complement that with the strengths of your team and they too will feel highly valued and give it their all. This model liberates you as the leader to spend more of your time coaching and developing your team.

Being an inclusive leader

I've been a student of great leadership over the years, particularly the last decade while I have been exploring the question of whether there are different dynamics between male and female leaders. My own observation is that great leadership has universal traits that are agnostic of gender, and while some traits have a higher likelihood of appearing in men and others in women, the cocktail for good leadership is the same. Great leadership traits are inclusive and integrated. Great leaders focus on bringing out the best in their team, they are authentic, strategic, and lead through forming holistic teams that problem solve together.

Although intuitively that makes sense, and scientifically it's proven, it's still not the prevalent norm in most companies. Reactive leadership tendencies are often more prevalent; leading through position, or leading through direction. You only need to look at the low employee engagement score averages across companies to see that's the case.

If you are reading this book I have high hopes that you are already an inclusive leader, or an interested or aspiring one, so first I want to reassure you this approach is valuable, tried and tested, and is the most successful approach (even if other old-school leaders tell you differently). I say this because in my career the journey to inclusive leadership has had its ups and downs. My leadership traits – such as collaboration, high integrity, honesty and strategic thinking – have not always been valued by other senior leaders, who built their leadership approach based on power and position. I've been told by some of these very senior reactive leaders that being tough is what is needed – 'you need to show them who's boss' – versus being collaborative and using relationships as a basis for co-creating outcomes.

When I work with my executive coaching clients, many of them can name both great and bad bosses. Generally great bosses brought out the best in them, and trusted, coached and empowered them. Bad bosses simply gave them tasks to do, not only setting the task but also how they did it, being prescriptive based on their own style. And if things went off track, there was plenty of criticism and blame to go around.

Because reactive and directive leaders have strong views on both the what and the how, they tend to surround themselves with people who look like them and think like them. You can spot them easily if you look at the make up of their leadership teams and their boards. Leaders who operate this way have a high propensity to stick to existing norms and practices.

The danger with forming teams of people who all think, act and look like you is group think. The group norms to a set of beliefs and paradigms that become embedded, so even when faced with new challenges they get processed the same old way. There are all too many examples of companies or organisations 'falling over' based on group think: the Challenger space shuttle disaster, Volkswagen emissions, Enron and Lehman Brothers are all famous examples. But many not so famous ones happen in senior leadership meetings in major corporations every single day.

In the past this approach was not necessarily a limiting one. Running businesses in the eighties and nineties with the main lens of shareholder value and a stable marketplace, this approach worked reasonably well. But we are far from a predictable and constant model now; we are living in a 'VUCA' world. Initially this appeared as a military acronym to categorise how conflict situations were shifting in **V**olatility, **U**ncertainty, **C**omplexity and **A**mbiguity. It's since been adopted in the business world to categorise shifts created by consumer changes, growing knowledge, information availability and digital connectedness, which are causing the business landscape to be constantly shifting and evolving. Listening to your consumers and customers and constant adaptability to changing conditions is needed. Leading in a VUCA world creates the mandate and business case for a change in leadership styles.

The only way to lead and stay on top of changes is to form teams with a broad spectrum of experience, knowledge and perspectives. Inclusive leaders form their teams very differently; they fundamentally believe that the more diverse the thinking and perspectives brought to the team the better the outcome, and they form their teams based on the challenges they are facing and the desired outcomes, not the tasks they want to tick off.

Diversity of thinking logically comes with diversity of teams. That diversity comes from an equal presence of men and women, different ages, different cultural backgrounds and different nationalities. The team created to solve a business challenge should reflect the customer or community you are trying to solve it for, otherwise how can you really predict and intuitively give them solutions that are in tune with their needs? This is the crux of the business case on gender diversity.

The good news is the case for change became clear, particularly on female diversity, and it became a strategic approach adopted by many businesses. Initial progress was made whereby the number of senior female leaders increased. The challenge is that number has stalled at around a third, and a *Harvard Business Review* article recently calculated that at the current rate of change it would take 250 years to get to gender parity in leadership positions. The reason this stall has happened is that the pipeline increased but the culture in organisations did not change. The prevalent style of leadership remains reactive rather than creative and inclusive. This was exacerbated by the Global Financial Crisis, which made corporations more risk averse and more likely to revert to the comfort zone of teams that look and think the same as the leaders.

When you look at it from an intellectual standpoint it clearly would make sense to increase the diversity of thinking applied to problem solving in changing and turbulent times. But that is not how our brain processes threats; instead organisations retreat and entrench tried and trusted approaches. This view is further validated by other studies that show that since the GFC the number of women in senior leadership positions has gone backwards rather than forwards.

Creating inclusive leaders and diverse teams

This issue is much bigger than gender; it is about inclusive leadership and thinking. So what should companies do about this? If you truly want to build inclusive leaders and diverse teams, these tips will harness the power of **With**:

- Make **creative and inclusive leadership** a non-negotiable: you can measure it; you can build it in teams.

- **Shake up how teams are formed** based on the nature of the business challenges you face. Define the problem clearly and form a team to fix it, rather than, 'Here's our team ... we will work out every problem'.

- Get good with **robust discussion and diverse perspectives**. Reframe this from being a challenge to great problem solving.

- **Throw out preconceived opinions** on age, gender, culture and ethnicity, and see each of these groups and each individual as a complete bundle of gifts and talents.

Teams that know each other and understand where each member of the team comes from form the best teams, because only through relationships can you build trust and mutual respect.

Being a true team doesn't happen automatically. When you are a leader what you have is a collection of direct reports, and in most cases people are promoted into a role and inherit their team. I find the best place to start is really getting to know each other. As a leader you will naturally start with one-on-one interactions. I find as a leader – particularly if your EQ is pretty high – you will be able to gain a good understanding of each person and what makes them tick, and by so doing bring out the best in them individually. But even if you manage to achieve that individually you still face the tricky task of how do you get this collective group of individuals to work well together?

Getting a group of people from different functions and backgrounds to pull together as a team just because they are united by you being their boss isn't going to happen naturally. You may get pockets of collaboration, but if your goal is cross functional, cross geography and cross cultural it may take some work. Getting to know each other is a great start, and when I say getting to know each other, not simply in your functional capacities (albeit that helps) but knowing each other well enough that you have common ground and can relate to each other.

WITH

The accepted wisdom on teams is that they need to go through forming, storming, norming, and performing. As a leader you can accelerate that path through how you lead the team to success.

UNLOCKING THE POWER OF TEAMS THROUGH IDEAS

One simple tool for recognising the individual skills each team member brings to the team is the IDEA model, which I picked up at a training program a few years back and have adapted and used since. It's a great yet simple model because it can be applied to teams, project management and problem solving to get you started. Let's have a look at it.

Each of your team members will tend to have one of the following attributes:

- **I** is about ideas and innovation. These are your team members who love brainstorming, they are always coming up with new ideas and different thinking angles, and they use language like, 'What if? … '

- **D** is about developing. These people thrive on taking ideas and developing them into something tangible. They look at an idea and take it to the next level. They are great at seeing what you would need to do to get from an idea to a plan.

- **E** is about evaluating. They are the people who will really figure out if something will work. Is it doable and financially viable?

- **A** is act. These are the people who get stuff done. They are the people who get projects implemented and out the door. They make things happen.

A high-performing team needs all these skills to succeed.

Take some time to reflect on your own team and place the team members into the IDEA framework. Take a look – is it balanced? Are you overrepresented in one type or another? And where do *you* sit?

Also through the lens of this model, think about the unique skills and gifts each team member brings. All four areas should have equal importance and a clear role. This gives value to each team member and averts negative comments within a team; for example, marketers getting frustrated with legal or finance for not approving something, while they are frustrated marketing haven't thought it through. But in reality, they all missed 'developing', and the teams did not respect each other's roles.

If you have a team of evaluators ideating, the projects can be too narrow in their scope and so safe as to not be game changing. Starting at 'E' without pushing the boundaries is therefore limiting.

Map a project through the stages. What should happen for your project at each stage in theory, using the model? Is that happening now, or is the project falling down in any area? Without having a balance of people in the team or following the steps, projects and teams can get stuck because they miss key steps and ideas are half baked.

If you have a team of innovative people, ideas are constantly flowing, but if you link them with the 'As' you go from idea to act. Given the idea wasn't honed and thought through by developers it can be expected to have some operational issues, and without evaluators it may not have financial and business rigour behind it. With this approach you end up burning resources on lots of projects that get to market but very few that are successful.

You get the idea – once you've mapped your team and your projects using this approach, work out what dynamic is playing out in your team, then work on the gaps.

> '**I actually realized I was more convincing to myself and to the people who were listening when I actually said what I thought, versus what I thought people wanted to hear me say.**'
>
> **Ursula Burns, CEO Xerox**

LIFE FINGERPRINT: WITH

Now you have gone through the **With** chapter, complete the Life Fingerprint on the next page.

Think firstly about your family, then your friends, and list the top five priority people and what aspect of the relationship is important. Then reflect on your colleagues – this time more as a collective 'with' – and determine what the attributes are of the kind of people you like to work with.

WITH
The important people in my life are?

Family (capture the who and what...)

1. _____
2. _____
3. _____
4. _____
5. _____

Friends (capture the who and what...)

1. _____
2. _____
3. _____
4. _____
5. _____

My Top 5 energy givers are...

1. _____
2. _____
3. _____
4. _____
5. _____

The attributes of colleagues I work best with are...

1. _____
2. _____
3. _____
4. _____
5. _____

LIFE FINGERPRINT

Sparks and Jolts

Sparks and Jolts

Chapter 5

<u>Why</u> ... do I do what I do?

FIND YOUR WHY

> 'Success is liking yourself, liking what you do, and liking how you do it.'
>
> **Maya Angelou**

There's a building 'movement' initiated by Simon Sinek with a call to action to 'Start with Why'. Sinek's talk about this on TED.com is the third most watched talk of all time, with over 30 million views. In that talk he lays out a compelling argument when referring to a company's approach that 'people don't buy what you do, they buy why you do it'. In my career I strove to build that ethos into how I led and how I built external partnerships by creating a shared **Why** with my teams and with partners, but as I worked more on unravelling how to build your best life and best career it struck me what better question can we pose to ourselves than 'why do I do what I do?'

> 'Here's to the crazy ones. The misfits. The rebels.
> The troublemakers. The round pegs in the square holes.
> The ones who see things differently. They're not fond of
> rules. And they have no respect for the status quo. You
> can quote them, disagree with them, glorify or vilify them.
> About the only thing you can't do is ignore them. Because
> they change things. They push the human race forward.
> And while some may see them as the crazy ones, we see
> genius. Because the people who are crazy enough to
> think they can change the world, are the ones who do.'
>
> **Rob Siltanen and Steve Jobs**

Defining your purpose or being clear on your **Why** is so important. With my coaching clients I can see and feel when people are passionate and purpose-led versus when they are not, and it makes a massive difference to how they feel about themselves and how they show up in life. I am sure you can spot it too in colleagues and friends. Compare talking to someone about what they love doing versus what they dislike doing and you can see that passion. They smile more, enthuse, and are energetic compared to talking about something they don't like, when they become purely descriptive about what they do, with no intonation in their voice and body language, and very low energy. These observations are very much in line with what we talked about in the section on sources of energy in the previous chapter. When talking about our areas of passion those areas come across as Energy Givers; when talking about things we don't enjoy they were defined at best as Energy Sloths and in most cases as Energy Vampires. If you just got a Spark that your career is a true Energy Giver to you, congratulations – you are in the happy minority! If your Spark was more of an, 'Oh no, I am truly in a Sloth- or Vampire-like state in my career', odds are you are not doing something that is line with your **Why** or purpose, and that needs attention …

> 'Don't become a wandering generality.
> Be a meaningful specific.'
>
> **Zig Ziglar**

When I first embarked on this journey to define purpose it sounded very idealistic, unrealistic and unattainable, and for a long time I wrestled with how best to define it for myself and then ultimately to help others do the same. What I settled on was that your purpose or your **Why** is found at the convergence of a few areas:

- **Your values:** The five areas that define your 'value set'.

- **Your strengths and skills:** What you are best at doing; what comes naturally to you.

- **Your beliefs:** What you really believe.

- **Your 'If money was no object':** How you would decide what you would do if this were the case.

- **Your gifts:** Your gifts are uniquely you, because they are a blend of who you are and what you are good at.

HOW ENGAGED ARE YOU IN YOUR JOB AND CAREER?

The idea of designing and building a career that brings out the best in you and is in tune with your **Why** intuitively makes sense, right? Why would you do it any other way? After all, when we are at our best we are more enthusiastic, more passionate about what we do, feel we are making a contribution, and feel we are operating with purpose.

I have found the number one determinant of how much people achieve in their role, and how happy and fulfilled they feel doing it, is how well what they do aligns with why they do it. The criteria for looking at this fit include:

- how well the requirements of the role match their skills and competencies

- how much they are true to their values

- how much they enjoy working with their boss and colleagues

- how much the organisational culture and style is in alignment with their operating style and values.

I will come back to how engaged we personally are with our career. First, let's take a look at how major companies measure engagement.

Measuring engagement

If you have a corporate role, employee engagement is probably a hot topic at your work, with engagement being measured as the emotional commitment you feel towards the organisation and its goals. You, like me, have no doubt filled in an annual employee engagement survey to measure this (in many cases, year after year …).

What companies rely on is employee engagement surveys to understand how engaged their employees are, you should intuitively know about and pay attention to yourself; for example, how emotionally committed are you? How much do you actually care about your work and your company? Attributes that indicate you are engaged in your work include you don't feel like you are working just for pay, or just for the next promotion, rather you are working there because you feel part of something bigger because your personal goals and those of the organisation converge.

The reason companies do employee engagement surveys is that it has been proven – and this will come as no big surprise – that engaged employees lead to better organisational results, such as:

- higher service, quality and productivity, which leads to …

- higher customer satisfaction, which leads to …

- increased sales (repeat business and referrals), which leads to …

- higher levels of profit, which leads to …

- higher shareholder returns (a higher stock price).

When you care about your job or career, you are engaged and you use your discretionary effort to do a better job. Not rocket science, correct? But remarkably, despite this immutable fact, the number of people who enjoy their role or career is much lower than you would think or hope …

Don't confuse engagement with being okay with your job. You may still be satisfied or even happy at work, but that doesn't necessarily mean you are working hard, productively, or you are feeling fully involved with your company. Feeling okay is quite frankly not okay. It's not enough. You can waste many a year with a company just being okay, when your expectation should be as a minimum feeling good – and ideally feeling great – about your job and career.

Here's how I have heard people justify why they are sticking with a job they don't feel engaged with:

- 'It pays the mortgage.'

- 'The people I work with are nice.'

- 'It's an easy commute from where I live.'

- 'It will get better.' (But they have been saying that for three years!)

- 'I think it's me; I need to try harder to fit in.'

If these are the reasons you use to justify to yourself staying where you are, quite frankly they are not good enough. In the long run, feeling like this versus really enjoying your role or career and it being in tune with your **Who**, **What**, **With**, and now **Why** will have a negative impact on your health, self-worth and level of achievement.

If you strive for having a great job or career, the only way to do it is to make sure that what you do is aligned with why you do it. If what we do for a living and how we show up at work is completely in tune with our passions and skills, we do our job much better, we are emotionally and visibly engaged, work feels easy, effortless and intuitive, and colleagues will comment on your positivity, creativity and can-do attitude. If that's already sounding like you, congratulations! You are one of the lucky minority of the working population. If you are reading this and thinking you are in the 'it's okay at work' camp, you are in the unfortunate majority.

Gallup, who specialise in employee engagement studies, found in their US study that only 32% of employees are engaged, 51% are not engaged, and 17% are actively disengaged. In Australia the stats are 32% of employees are engaged, 51% are not engaged, and 16% are actively disengaged.

Gallup's employee engagement research found that there is a direct relationship between low workplace engagement and the prevalence of negative emotions among employees worldwide. They found the results to be particularly strong in Australia and New Zealand. Almost half of actively disengaged workers in Australia and New Zealand (47%) admitted to having experienced stress for much of the previous day, while 24% experienced sadness, and 20% experienced anger. Although clearly engaged people feel these same emotions at work (26%, 11% and 8% respectively), the stress and health impacts of regularly feeling disengaged at work will take a toll on you. It is not sustainable.

Gallup also found there has to be alignment between employees' roles and why they do them and the organisation's mission. In the Australian companies Gallup studied, they found that only 22% of workers strongly agreed that the mission and purpose of their company makes them feel their job is important. They also found that line managers can improve this metric by asking employees to articulate what they get paid to do, what success looks like in their role, and whether they have what they need to achieve success. These questions are good ones to ask yourself and your team. A core part of your individual and collective **Why** with a company is knowing that individually and collectively you feel your contributions connect to the wider company mission and goals of your company.

> 'What I know is that if you do work that you love, and the work fulfils you, the rest will come.'
>
> **Oprah Winfrey**

Given all of this, the goal is to build a job and career completely in tune with your passions and skills, where you are emotionally and actively engaged, where work feels easy, effortless and intuitive, and where those around you feel and sense your positivity, creativity and passion coming through. To really crack the code on this we need to spend some time thinking about our purpose at work, and what purpose work and career have for us. The following exercise is designed to uncover this.

WHAT ARE YOUR TRUE GIFTS?

Far more valuable than focusing on how we could be *more* is focusing on how we can regard ourselves as being *enough*. Every client and team member I have met and coached has something to bring to the world, something they do, a skill, an ability, a passion. These are their true gifts that emerge from their Life Fingerprint. But what I also see is we so often keep our gifts hidden because we don't see them in ourselves, because we feel they may not be relevant or useful or that they don't meet the norms or expectations of others. But keeping those gifts under wraps means we are keeping ourselves under wraps. Then what happens?

We choose a path well travelled or 'normal' that doesn't play directly to our strengths and passions and therefore we are not as passionate about it, which means we don't give it our all. This means we don't always feel we do a great job, which means we become frustrated at ourselves for not being good enough and frustrated about how we are judged by others, which means we then say we are not good enough and need to work harder.

> 'There is no greater thing you can do with your life and your work than follow your passions – in a way that serves the world and you.'
>
> **Richard Branson**

SYNERGY: DISCOVERING YOUR GIFTS AND WHY EXERCISE

The first six exercises and frameworks in Life Design will help you with this, especially Life Line, Values, Strengths, and Inspiration, alongside Energy sources and Life Wheel. If you sped through these you can go back and do those exercises and then bring them back into play as part of discovering your gifts and your **Why**.

SYNERGY: DISCOVERING YOUR GIFTS AND YOUR WHY

The following pages have the framework you need to work this through. Sometimes people get a bit stuck on the 'I believe' part. Imagine this is a bit like the Martin Luther King 'I have a dream' speech. These are statements of beliefs you navigate your life by. Don't worry about whether they fit with your career or if you don't have as many as five, just capture what comes naturally. Examples include:

- 'I believe anything is possible if you put your mind to it.'

- 'I believe whether you believe you can or you can't, you are right.'

- 'I believe everyone has the right to be heard.'

- 'I believe in making a difference.'

- 'I believe family comes first.'

- 'I believe loyalty to my job and company comes first.'

- 'I believe making money is the most important thing in your career.'

You get the idea.

Defining your Why or purpose

Focus areas to discover your why	What I know about myself ...
Values *(Top 5)* Input to come from the top 5 values exercise	
Strengths *(Top 5)* Input to come from the top 5 strengths exercise	
My Top 5 'I Believe' statements are ...	
Gifts What do other people (boss, friends, colleagues) say you uniquely do?	
If I was unconstrained (by money, other people or my own thoughts), the area that would make me the happiest and most fulfilled would be ...	
My Why is... Your **Why** statement reflects what you do to positively impact the people around you...	*To ... (contribution) ...... so that ... (impact) ......*

What I know about myself ...

Finding your gifts

The most critical part of career planning comes at the convergence of your values, strengths and passions: these are your gifts. Gifts are tremendously important, because they define what skills you bring to your work that are uniquely you. They are the areas that you are naturally good at, and when you are doing projects in alignment with these they come really easily and naturally to you. The challenge with gifts is that we often find them difficult to see or appreciate in ourselves. They are often a blind spot for us. This is because they are so intuitive to us that we brush them off as not unique, making comments such as, 'Everybody does that, don't they?', or, 'I don't know how I do that – I just can.'

So if our gifts are often hidden from us, how do we find them? The answer lies in whether you are able to find patterns in your values, strengths and beliefs. If you struggle with this then you can discover your gifts with the help of other people who see and recognise those skills and gifts in you. These are the areas where other people come to you for advice or to lead a project, or to do something because they recognise that you do it better than anyone else. In many cases these areas may not even be core to your role, but people ask you anyway.

Here are a few examples from some recent leadership workshops. In each case the person didn't recognise the gift as unique to them, until colleagues stressed how unique and valued those skills were:

- 'I love leading projects. My boss comes to me to lead projects outside of my normal role because as well as making sure the project is delivered on time, I really enjoy engaging with all the different departments and functions and helping them see where they fit and are valued within the project, hearing their concerns and then addressing them. Even the unions, which most people find challenging, I manage in this way, and that's helped me manage complex change projects without industrial disputes.'

  Gift: 'Now I think about it ... I am the best in my company at managing projects because I combine my skills as an engineer with a love of engaging people in the project.'

- 'My boss always comes to me to capture the annual HR plan on a page. They talk about all the different areas that are important to us and the goals and hand me a big presentation that explains it.

I am able to summarise that in a simple summary that everyone in the team can understand and engage with. I can just see what needs to be done.'

Gift: 'Now I think about it ... although that has nothing to do with my normal role, and there are many others in the team, I am always asked to do this. I have realised I have a natural ability to simplify large amounts of information into something simple and easy to understand.'

- 'I am a project leader in a really complex organisation with lots of functions, stakeholders, egos and politics. I engage each person in turn and can see what they are really good at and bring to the team, plus I see what people's concerns are and objections are to getting the project done. That helps me navigate my projects to get agreement to go ahead, whereas my colleagues' projects seem to fall over.'

  Gift: 'Now I think about it ... I can see I get really complex projects through where others don't. I see all the skills in the project team and what they all bring to the table, and I can naturally see how to harness them for the good of the project. Team members tell me that they most enjoy working on the projects I lead, because I recognise and bring the best out in them.'

Hopefully these examples will have triggered some of your own thinking and you are able to capture some of your gifts. If you are still struggling with this, particularly those of you who may be your own worst critic, I suggest you engage and ask other people about it ... the people you really trust and whose opinion you value. Although I call them gifts because that's what they are, asking others what your gifts are is not the way to go ... I suggest instead that you let them know you are seeking to learn more about how you make the most of what you are best at and you'd like their opinion on what they see as your greatest strengths (**What**), and what it is about the way you do things that makes them pick that particular area (**How**).

Once you have defined your gifts you can try to navigate your career direction to make the most of these. That will help you make the most of your career, be your best and love what you do. If, on the other hand, you realise that you are in a job that doesn't play to your values, strengths and gifts, perhaps it's time to create a career shift!

WHY

YOUR <u>WHY</u> STATEMENT

After you have worked out these components it's easier to get to your **Why** statement. Returning to Simon Sinek's inspiration on this, he frames a **Why** statement to reflect what you do to positively impact the people around you:

To ... [your contribution] .... so that ... [your impact] ....

Richard Branson summed up similar thinking in this poem. His advice was to budding entrepreneurs but it equally applies to how we think about our career in business:

Screw it, let's do it

The road to success is paved with tests,
So you've got to believe in yourself above the rest.
Dream big, and let your passion shine,
If you don't, you won't end up with a dime.
Challenge the status quo, disrupt the market and say YES!
And remember that innovation is an endless quest.
Don't forget to change business for good,
If you want to change the world then you should.
If you think with your head and listen to your heart,
I promise you'll get off to a flying start.
Make bold moves, but always play fair,
Always say please and thank you – it's cool to care.
Do what you love and love what you do,
This advice is nothing new.
Now, stop worrying about whether your business will be a hit,
Rise to the challenge and say 'screw it, let's do it!'

LIFE FINGERPRINT: WHY

Pause now to reflect on your **Why**, and complete the next part of your Life Fingerprint. Capture your gifts and your top 'I believe' statements.

WHY
do I do what I do?

_____

My Top 5 'I believe' statements are...

1 _____

2 _____

3 _____

4 _____

5 _____

My unique gifts are... (Top 1–3)

1 _____

2 _____

3 _____

If I was unconstrained (by money, other people or my own thoughts...) and could do anything I wanted for the rest of my life, the area that would make me the most fulfilled would be...

_____

Your Why statement reflects what you do to positively impact the people around you...

To... (contribution)

_____

_____

so that... (impact)

_____

_____

Sparks and Jolts

Chapter 6

<u>Where</u> ... What places bring out the best in you?

Of all the 6Ws, the **Where** for most people doesn't get much attention compared to the weightier Ws of **Who, With, What** and **Why**. However, for a complete picture and full Life Design the **Where** part of the fingerprint has, in my experience, a significant part to play in your overall wellbeing.

Where has three main components that should be considered and captured in your Life Fingerprint:

- your home

- your environment and surroundings

- your work environment.

Let's have a look at each of these.

YOUR HOME

Defining and living in the right environment for who you are is key, and just a simple exercise of capturing the top five attributes of your home, particularly as you move house, will give more focus to your search for what works.

Take me as an example; I realised my home – and for me, even more importantly my garden – is a big driver of my happiness. I lived in rented accommodation for eight years after leaving the UK; great houses, but they didn't feel like home. I realised how much I needed to create a home, and it was a big part of my family life – being in the right home is a big energiser for me. As I moved back from living overseas in Malaysia to Australia I had a mood board on Pinterest (I realise for some people this will be a step too far …) for what my ideal house looks like: that I can see trees and garden through every window, that we are not overlooked, that I can get to the beach within 30 minutes, and it has good amenities and a great school within 15 minutes.

For other people my brief would be their worst nightmare as a place to live, and instead they may want a city apartment in the thick of all the action, with restaurants at their doorstep and great transport links to get them to work.

Whatever your brief is, list it on the Fingerprint, and then compare the brief to your reality.

YOUR ENVIRONMENT AND SURROUNDINGS

Following on from the home, the environment you are in is also important. In my case I need to be surrounded by nature not buildings – quiet versus busy.

What possessions do you like around you? What pictures are on your wall? Do you prefer a modern or historical environment?

What does *your* ideal look like?

YOUR WORK ENVIRONMENT

Given how long we spend at work, having a brief for the work environment is important too. The lens on this can be 'organisational and work environment'. Here's some thought starters to get you going, so you can complete the Fingerprint:

- Hierarchical or egalitarian?

- Diverse or people like you?

Where ... What places bring out the best in you?

- Traditional or constantly changing?

- Formal or informal?

- Indoors or outdoors?

- Travel or no travel?

LIFE FINGERPRINT: WHERE

Pause now to reflect on your **Where**, and complete the next part of your Life Fingerprint on the following page. Capture what is important about your home and work environments, and where you like to unwind.

WHERE
What places bring out the best in me?

My home (list the important attributes)

1. _____
2. _____
3. _____
4. _____
5. _____

My environment and surroundings

1. _____
2. _____
3. _____
4. _____
5. _____

My work environment

1. _____
2. _____
3. _____
4. _____
5. _____

If I want to relax and unwind the ideal place to do that is... and why?

_____

_____

_____

Sparks and Jolts

Sparks and Jolts

Chapter 7

<u>When</u> ... is the right time?

I'm often asked how people should decide **When** is the right time to do things in life: to focus on their career, to have children, to prioritise relationships or family, to prioritise work. As you will have gathered by now, all the Ws are highly interdependent – the **When** and **Where** naturally follow after **Who**, **What**, **With** and **Why**.

Gaining clarity on both goals and their timing is where you start to integrate the ongoing practice of living your best life. Let's begin by looking at how you stay in tune with your environment to help you make decisions about **When** for career choices.

> 'As soon as something stops being fun, I think it's time to move on. Life is too short to be unhappy. Waking up stressed and miserable is not a good way to live.'
>
> **Richard Branson**

LOVE IT, LIKE IT, LEARN FROM IT, LAUGH ABOUT IT OR LEAVE IT

I have developed a very simple philosophy to test whether you are in the right role now and when you should change. This will enable you to evaluate if current and future roles are right for you.

The approach I take is … Love it, Like it, Learn from it, Laugh about it or Leave it. Let's see how it works:

- Let's start with **Love it** and **Like it**. This is when you feel that the job you are doing is great, it brings out the best in you, the work environment suits you, and you feel trusted, empowered and valued. That should be your goal. If this is not how you are feeling about your career, pay attention to it and fix it.

- **Learn from it** roles are pretty important on your career path. At the end of the day, to thrive in your career and ultimately be a great leader, a breadth of experience really helps. Some roles you should stay in to help build your knowledge and competencies. Such roles do this by putting you outside your comfort zone, shifting your environment or placing you in an area you are not the subject matter expert in. In some cases people learn so much they make a career shift to stay in this area, particularly if they come to love it. If not, you can move from these roles back into Love it roles with better knowledge and more experience that will help you perform those roles even better.

- **Laugh about it** may seem an odd definition for a role, but sometimes laughter is the best remedy. How you feel about a role can change based on the level of challenge or uncertainty in the business environment. In the corporate environment a successful year can be followed by one where the market shifts and growth is hard to achieve. When you are not hitting the numbers, if you don't pay attention to it the work environment can shift to fear, blame, stress and negativity. To try to get results back on track the hours are long, the frustration and uncertainty are high, and work relationships can grow tense and challenging.

  In my experience, these negative behaviours don't fix anything. But if you apply a learn and laugh mindset, things shift. Humour creates the right path to the problem solving part of your brain, and releases endorphins that help you cope better with what life throws at you. So in some roles, where there is a crisis, just hang in there and form a tight link with your close work buddies and problem solve while keeping the work environment upbeat, positive and supportive of each other, with a fair bit of humour or 'banter' thrown in to diffuse stressful situations. After the stress has passed and the business is back on track, you will have learnt from it too.

- The last type of role is a **Leave it** role. These roles typically started out as a Love, Like, Learn or Laugh role, but if none of these conditions prevail, it is time to leave. I observe far too many people staying in roles they don't enjoy and that are slowly but surely chipping away at their passion, confidence and self-esteem. I see many of my coaching clients shut down their greatest strengths or lose sight of their values, and they are just going through the motions. This is a dangerous cycle, because you become disengaged, then you do a worse job, then your self-esteem and ego are further hit.

Pay attention to your roles and career path. If a position is not working for you after you have really given it your best shot, it might be time to shift to something different.

If you pay attention and spot problems early, leaving a role can be easier than you think. You might spot a role in another department, you can look at what's on the market, and you can actively pursue other roles until you find the right one and move on. This orchestrated, purposeful approach works really well; it's all part of career planning. But all too often this is not what I observe. People stick in there, become fed up, feel stressed, get negative, complain to others – these are the attributes I highlighted earlier in the section on engagement. If you have become disengaged it also becomes harder to secure the next role, because how you are showing up as negative.

If this is where you think you are, revisit your 6Ws, and reconnect with **Who** you are and your **Why**. You need to be in a positive space to address it; it's hard to build anything from a point of negativity.

THE GOOD, THE BAD AND THE UGLY ABOUT HOW BOSSES IMPACT YOUR CAREER

The Love it, Like it, Learn from it, Laugh about it or Leave it approach is also a good way to assess what you do about the good, the bad and the ugly lessons from bosses.

WHEN

When do you stay?

When do you go?

Exit interviews have shown the number one reason people leave a role or organisation is because of their boss, and based on my own experience that is often the case, however not always. In my case the decision to leave my corporate career and set up my own business was all about my passions and gifts and nothing to do with my boss; when I left I was working for a boss I loved working for.

Good bosses are responsible for being a great leader to us, giving us coaching, assessing our performance so they can help us grow, giving us support and advice, helping us learn, stretching us to reach our potential but not pushing us so far we fall over. But bosses can also be the dark side of all these traits: critical, demanding, stretching us beyond our limits. They are in many cases the makers or breakers of career success.

When I was writing this chapter, I counted up all my bosses and mapped them out, capturing their impact on me. What I found was that over my 30-year corporate career I had 17 direct bosses: six I loved working for, seven I liked working for, and four I didn't like working for so I orchestrated a Leave … Interestingly, I learned from every single one of them something I took with me into my own leadership, because I paid attention to what I thought was great about how they operated and also what I thought didn't work … both were great learnings.

> 'I learned to always take on things I'd never done before. Growth and comfort do not coexist.'
>
> **Virginia M. Rometty**

I would encourage you to map out your bosses too. You will find patterns in how you rate them and what attributes they have that cause you to regard them in that way. In my case a pattern emerged when I reflected back on my values (as you will have captured in the exercise in chapter 2); I discovered my main reason was how their value set compared to mine. In bosses I wanted to 'Leave' their values were very different to mine, and that was what was driving my discomfort. In the bosses I loved and liked working for our value set was always aligned, but the differentiator for loved versus liked was in how they helped me grow and learn and stretch my thinking.

As you build your career, navigating towards working for the types of bosses you like or love working for will help you build your own capabilities and leadership. Staying working for those you don't like working for will – in my experience – make you unhappy and make you want to leave.

I'm often asked how to navigate away from those 'bad' bosses. The answer is, with a plan ... spot it early, make sure you are not relying on your boss for your career by building your own networks you can call on, and orchestrate a role in another department or team. You can usually live with it for a while, so no need for snap decisions ... but if you spot that it's not working, initiate the plan and take control. All the bosses I didn't connect with and who were my 'leave' bosses appear as the work low points on my lifeline; once you realise that, you know you have no choice but to act.

INTEGRATION

Having already completed Synthesis and Synergy tools, you have now reached the last phase: including the **When** and **Where** parts of the jig-saw to drive integration into a forward life plan for action. One aspect of **When** is driven by the career choices you navigate through Love it, Like it, Learn from it, Laugh about it or Leave it. Another significant choice for both **When** and **Where** is driven by **Who** you want to live your life **With**, and **What** future milestones you have.

WRITING YOUR BIOGRAPHY AND LIVING YOUR AUTOBIOGRAPHY

To take that thought a step further: if you are still wondering whether you should carry on living your life as you are or focus on Best Life Design, ponder what you want your reflections to be on your deathbed. I don't want to dwell on this for long, but I find the stark reality of projecting yourself to the end of your life and thinking about what you want your life to have stood for gives you a massive shake up and creates a stark realisation that there are a few things that need to change.

My own observations are backed up by plenty of research. Consistent studies have shown that as people come to the end of their life they

WHEN

start feeling sadness and regret for what they didn't do, achieve, share with others, or say. Hopefully that end point is significantly far away, however if your goal is that you don't want this to happen to you, start living your best life now.

> 'You have Brains in your Head. You have feet in your shoes. You can steer yourself any direction you choose.'
>
> **Dr Seuss**

As an input to your thoughts, I wanted to share something that inspired me to think this way. Bronnie Ware is an author who was an Australian palliative care nurse who spent several years caring for patients in their homes in the last three to twelve weeks of their lives. She recorded their dying epiphanies and turned this into an article and then a book called *The Top 5 Regrets of the Dying** – the themes were:

1. I wish I'd had the courage to live a life true to myself, not the life others expected of me.
2. I wish I hadn't worked so hard.
3. I wish I'd had the courage to express my feelings.
4. I wish I had stayed in touch with my friends.
5. I wish that I had let myself be happier.

> 'The regrets touch upon being more genuine, not working so hard, expressing one's true feelings, staying in touch with friends and finding more joy in life.'
>
> **Bronnie Ware**

I came to the principle of Best Life Design through the goal of living your life to the full with no regrets at the end. Through living your life true to your 6Ws Fingerprint I believe this is possible. So with that in mind I would encourage you now to map your life forward as if you were writing your future biography and autobiography – it will add further strong guidance to how you map the **When** and **Where** of your life.

---

* For more information about Bronnie Ware and *The Top 5 Regrets of the Dying* visit hayhouse.com.au or bronnieware.com.

INTEGRATION:
AUTOBIOGRAPHY AND BIOGRAPHY

Consistent studies have shown that as people come to the end of their life they start feeling sadness and regret for what they did not do, achieve, share with others, or say. Hopefully that end point is significantly far away, however if your goal is that you don't want this to happen to you, you should start living your best life now. This exercise aims to help you think this through more clearly.

Reflect on your life like it was an autobiographical book (you were writing it about yourself); what would the recent and future chapters of your autobiography be? Think also about those people you are living your life with.

YOUR AUTOBIOGRAPHY
AND BIOGRAPHY

As we build out an integrated forward-looking plan for our lives, a powerful way to do this is to think in autobiographical terms. Starting from your current age, make each chapter 10 years. Instead of looking back as we did in the Life Line exercise, try to envisage your forward plans through the lens of **When**, **Where**, **What**, **With**, **Who** and **Why**. The Autobiography and Biography exercises on the next few pages will help you work this through.

My Autobiography

Starting from your current age, make each chapter 10 years. Instead of looking back as we did in the Life Line exercise, try

Chapter	WHEN (age)	WHERE (location)	WHAT are you doing?
Thought starters		• Home town • Other countries	• Marriage, family • Capture milestones such as retirement, or children leaving home
1	30–39		
2	40–49		
3	50–59		
4	60–69		
5	70+		

to envisage your forward plans through the lens of **When, Where, What, With, Who** and **Why.**

WITH – Who are the key people around you? How did they make you feel?	WHO am I and WHY am I doing it? (Think about what your drivers/values were and the highs and lows)
• Relationships • Husband/Wife • Friends • Children	• Capture how your values and priorities shift • Stressful job • Goals for retirement

WHEN

From the Autobiography exercise, capture your observations

What are the key milestones you can see in the future?

Capture any other observations you make:

Did your values change or stay consistent over time?

Did any past milestones shape how you thought or felt; for example, family, relationships, jobs?

How easy was it to think about what you want in the future ?

Integrate into a planned biography

Now think about your life as if it was a biography on you written by others you care about; what would you want them to say about what you did together and how they feel about you?

Firstly, define one to three people you want to create a biography for; these are people you care about deeply enough that what they think and feel about you is core to your life. Examples include:

- your partner
- your children
- your parents
- your friends
- your team.

Secondly, what do you want them to say or feel about you? Examples include:

- inspiring
- caring
- there for me
- thoughtful
- I trust them
- learning
- exploring
- great fun
- great sense of humour.

My Biography

Using the same chapter breaks you set in your autobiography and keeping the **Where** and **When** consistent, look at your life through the lens of what recent memories you have created

Chapter	WHEN (age)	WITH/WHAT (Capture both the key people and groups, what you are doing together, and what memories you would want them to have of you.)
Thought starters		WITH: Choose 1 to 3 priorities from your partner, your children, your parents, your friends, your team. Capture a memory of WHAT you did that you would like to read in their biography of you. *Examples:* Team: Set clear vision and supported us achieving our goals. *Child:* We always had great trips exploring together. *Partner:* Our trips together travelling are our happiest.
1	30–39	
2	40–49	
3	50–59	
4	60–69	
5	70+	

and what future memories you would want to create with your key people. Reflect on how you would want to be remembered in their biography about you. Bear in mind both their age and yours.

WHO am I and WHY am I doing it? (Drawing on who you are as reflected in your autobiography, capture the impact of your future life priorities on other people.)

Given WHO you are (as reflected in your Life Line, Values and Strengths) combined with WHY you do what you do to contribute to others, capture how you would like them to think and feel about the memory.

Examples: Team: Great coach who helped me see potential in myself. *Child:* Helped me define my values and believe in myself. *Partner:* After all the years focusing on the kids, we became as close as we were when we got married.

WHEN

From the Biography exercise, capture your observations

Did the exercise help you think through how others see you? Does it change how you see yourself? Capture your thoughts.

Capture any other observations you made:

Did your values show up differently or the same for each person you chose? How?

If that biography was truly going to be what they said and felt about you, what things do you need to focus on in your future life plan? Capture your top five actions:

1.

2.

3.

4.

5.

INTEGRATING CHANGE INTO YOUR LIFE

So now you have thought through what practical steps you'd like to make in your life and career, you can make steps and adjustments to integrate them into your Best Life Design. What I have found both in my own personal experience and with clients is that integration is key, combining the shifts and adjustments you want to make with the aspects of your life you are happy with. Focusing first on the aspects of your life you want to make the biggest adjustment to (as measured by the Life Wheel exercise and the 12-month integration plan) and clustering opportunities together (adding a **What** to a **With** to a **When** …) creates maximum impact. Choosing your time horizons too will give it some priority – *what now?* What do I want to do in the next year? And for each major milestone after that?

I have found people get the best traction if they start by choosing a handful of things that matter most to them in the next six months. For recent coaching clients that included:

- making a shift in my career to a new job that plays to my strengths

- returning to study

- arranging travel to a cultural destination I love

- paying attention to my health and diet

- finding a partner

- finding some 'me' time to visit museums and galleries.

As you can see from the list, these are tweaks and adjustments – each area really doesn't take much time. But in every case these were areas that were really important to each person, and an area they felt was really important to how they felt about life. And in every case they felt that, despite this, they had neglected it.

> 'You can have it all. Just not all at once.'
>
> **Oprah Winfrey**

WHEN

Clustering and finding synergy is very effective in getting the most out of life. One of my clients loved walking and being outdoors, loved great food, and wanted to spend more time with their partner because they were both flat out at work. They arranged a walking holiday, followed by a few days in a wine region with great restaurants, and decided to travel just the two of them rather than with their children for those few days so they could spend quality time together. Three life integration boxes ticked, and one great holiday later their Life Wheel was already feeling a bit less wonky!

These examples sound so simple – surely it takes something more radical or a massive rethink to design your best life? But honestly, no it doesn't. What I have found is a few tweaks and adjustments and a bit of planning go a long way. After all, your life was probably okay before and you just needed to make that nudge to make it great; it's about optimisation.

This works for the low-hanging fruit, but you are right to think that everything isn't that simple. Career shifts, relationship shifts and lifestyle shifts take more time and concerted effort, but the principle of change remains the same. You just need to decide it's important. Think it through and create a plan. If you don't do these things, nothing will change … That's the essence of *Think. Plan. Live.*

The following exercises on milestone planning will help. Choose one or two milestone shifts you want to work through and then do the exercises to help figure out the balance the eight Life Wheel areas would need to make that a reality.

> '80% of what you planned for is better than
> 100% of what you didn't plan for … '
>
> **Gill McLaren**

INTEGRATION INTO A FORWARD LIFE PLAN: NEXT 12 MONTHS

■ A clearer picture will be emerging through the lens of **Who**, **What**, **With** and **Why**. This, combined with clarity about what you want to focus on in your Life Wheel, forms the foundations of the Life Plan.

■ You are now ready for the first phase of integration into a forward Life Plan. We will start with the next 12 months and capture the actions and practical steps you want to take.

■ Using the outputs from the Life Wheel exercise, you can set goals and build a 12-month action plan.

■ Define the actions and then their priority for each aspect of the Life Wheel for the next 12 months, capture the top actions required, and decide how important (1 to 8) that aspect is in the next 12 months; for example, my top priority is career and deciding what my next job move is, and my actions are x, y, z.

■ Allow at least one hour to complete this exercise.

Life Plan: 1 year

Life category	Top three actions to focus on by category
Career and work	
Financial security and money	
Health and wellbeing	
Family and friends	
Relationship and romance	
Personal growth	
Fun and recreation	
Physical environment	

Actions for next 12 months	Priority rank 1–8 for next 12 months

WHEN

After you have completed your 12-month action plan, you are ready to map these priorities on the Life Plan on pages 188–189. Map the most important areas from your prioritisation grid. Think of the lens of **What**, **Where** and **With**:

- **What**: for example, career scope, business set up, health

- **Where**: for example, staying in current location, moving country, travel

- **With**: for example, partner, children, close friends (name), my family (name), by myself (include socialising and travel milestones).

Using these priorities, capture the key milestones you want to achieve.

To maximise your time, look for areas of convergence between the **What**, **Where** and **With**: for example, I want to travel and explore new cultures (**What**); I am keen to explore X because (**Where**); I want to go with my family, my friends, by myself ... (**With**).

Map out the plan to avoid multiple peaks and overlaps in time; for example, launch new business, pick up a challenging new project at work, take up yoga, travel ...

Notes

Life Plan: 1 year example

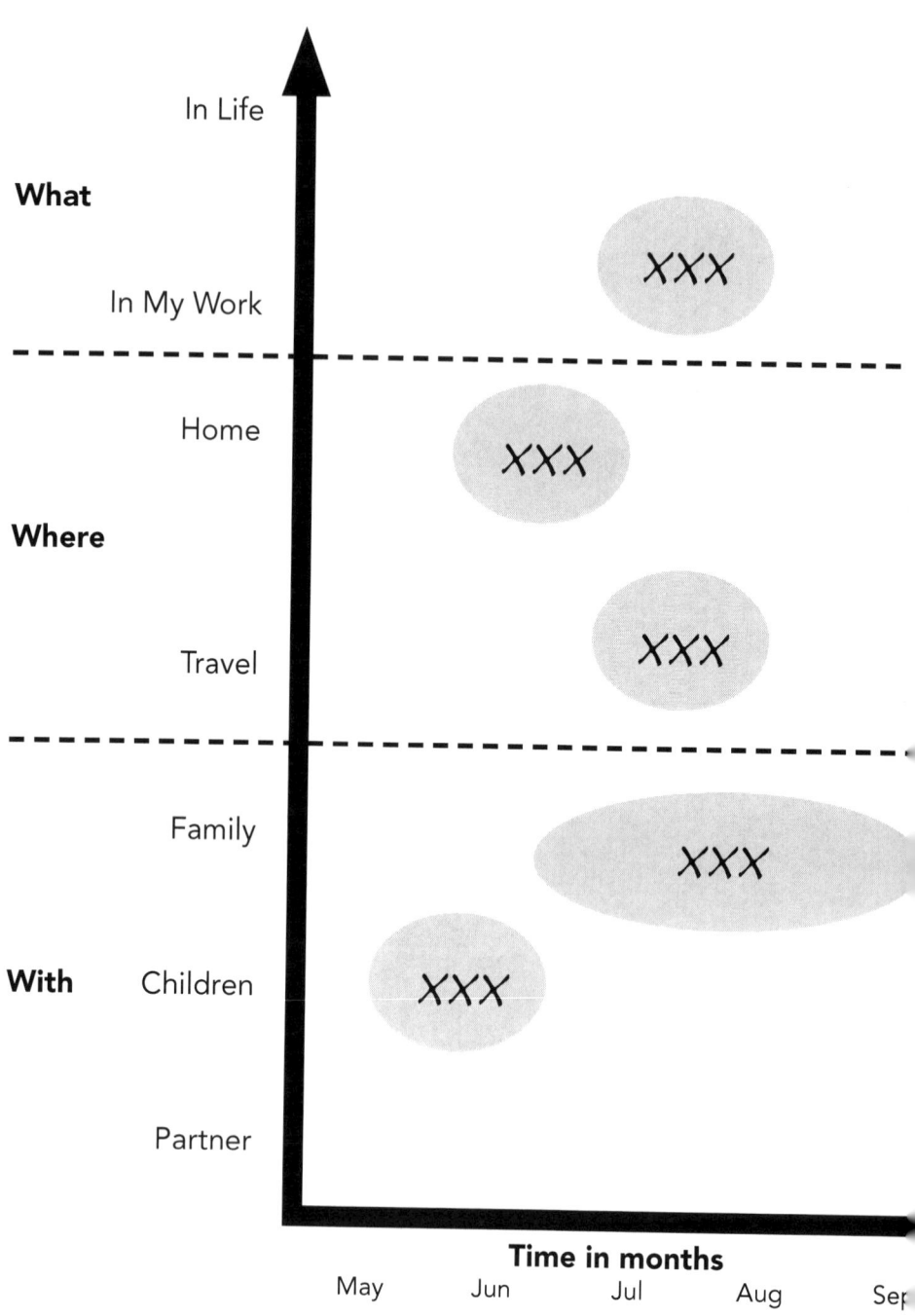

LIFE PLAN: 1 YEAR

XXX

XXX

Insert the key events and milestones

XXX

Oct   Nov   Dec   Jan   Feb   Mar   Apr

LIFE PLAN: 1 YEAR

Life Plan: 1 year

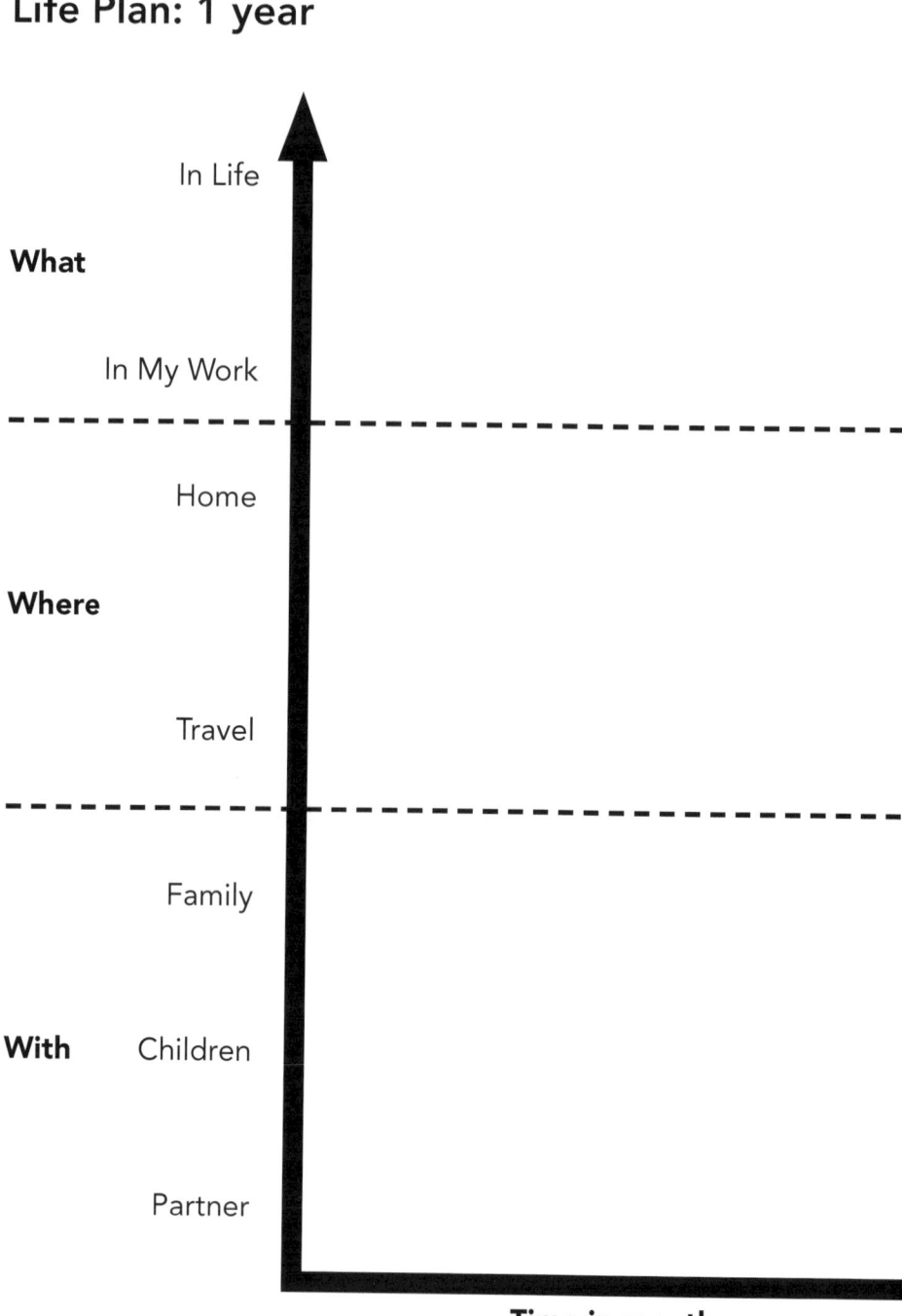

What
- In Life
- In My Work

Where
- Home
- Travel

With
- Family
- Children
- Partner

Time in months

LIFE PLAN: 1 YEAR

Draw your own 'bubbles' on the chart to capture the most important areas from your prioritisation grid.

 Insert the key events and milestones

WHEN

INTEGRATION INTO A FORWARD LIFE PLAN: MILESTONES EXERCISE

You now have completed the 12-month Life Plan using your 6Ws and what you want to address and change in your Life Wheel. You have also completed the My Biography and Autobiography step, which will have highlighted key people and key milestone events in the future you want to plan for.

You are now ready to integrate that into a forward life plan for you and to define a clear pathway to help you achieve significant milestone events or turning points you see ahead of you. Based on what other clients have worked towards, such milestones could be:

- retirement
- moving country; for example, if you have been living overseas
- children's learning; for example, study milestones, leaving home/ going to uni
- career progression or change goal
- moving location/house
- planning for aging parents.

INTEGRATION INTO A FORWARD LIFE PLAN: MILESTONES EXERCISE

Input into the Milestones Exercise should come from all your previous exercises, and bring that into a forward plan that reflects you, in particular:

- your 6Ws

- your Life Wheel reflections

- your completed 12-month Life Plan

- your completed Biography and Autobiography, which will have highlighted key people and key milestone events you want to plan for.

Step 1: Define key milestone events you want to plan for. Start with one significant event and then choose the next, but have no more than three in total.

Step 2: For each milestone you choose, look closely at the Life Wheel prioritisation; depending on the milestones, the relative importance of the actions changes.

Step 3: Using the table on the following pages define the actions and their priority for each aspect of the Life Wheel.

Step 4: Allow a minimum of one hour per milestone to complete this exercise; after all, this is the rest of your life we are talking about, so it's well worth spending time on.

Life Plan: key milestones

Life category	Top three actions to focus on by category
Career and work	
Financial security and money	
Health and wellbeing	
Family and friends	
Relationship and romance	
Personal growth	
Fun and recreation	
Physical environment	

Actions for this milestone	Priority rank 1–8 for this milestone

As you create your plan on a page for each milestone event you have identified, to ensure you are focusing on the most important areas of your life, firstly list your priority **What**, **Where** and **With**:

- **What**: for example, career, business, health, retire

- **Where**: for example, where do I live? Will I travel?

- **With**: for example, partner, children, close friends (name), my family (name), by myself (include socialising and travel milestones).

Using these priorities, capture the key milestones you want to achieve in your long term Life Plan. Think about your age and what milestones you want to achieve by what age.

Map each milestone on the next Life Plan on pages 198–201. The greatest benefit and synergy is seen when you merge the milestone maps together; for example, children's education with where you live with your next career move. The greater the synergy the more chance you have that your priorities complement rather than compete with each other.

Notes

WHEN

Life Plan: key milestones example

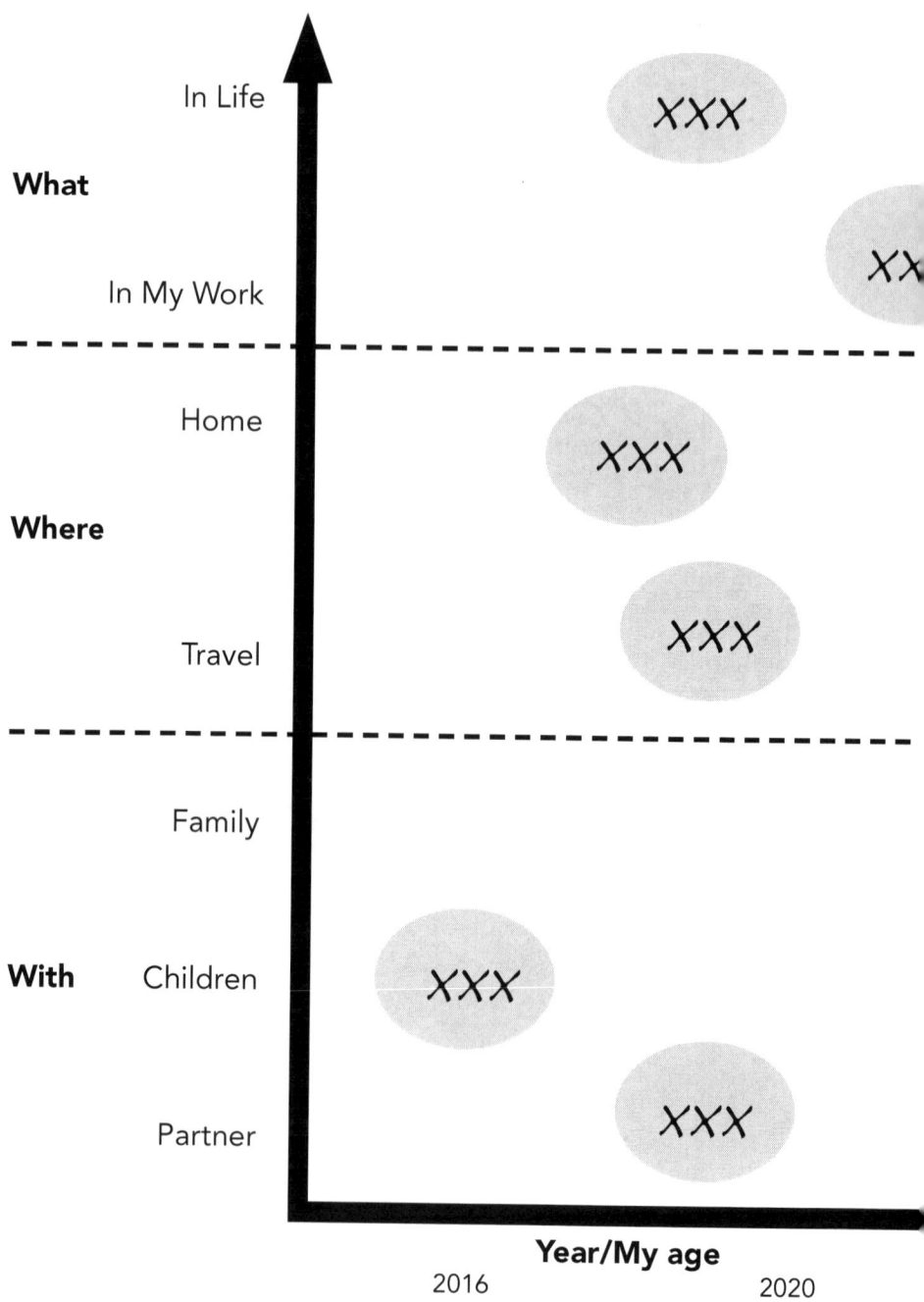

LIFE PLAN: MILESTONES

Insert the key events and milestones

xxx

2025 2030 2035+

Life Plan: key milestone 1

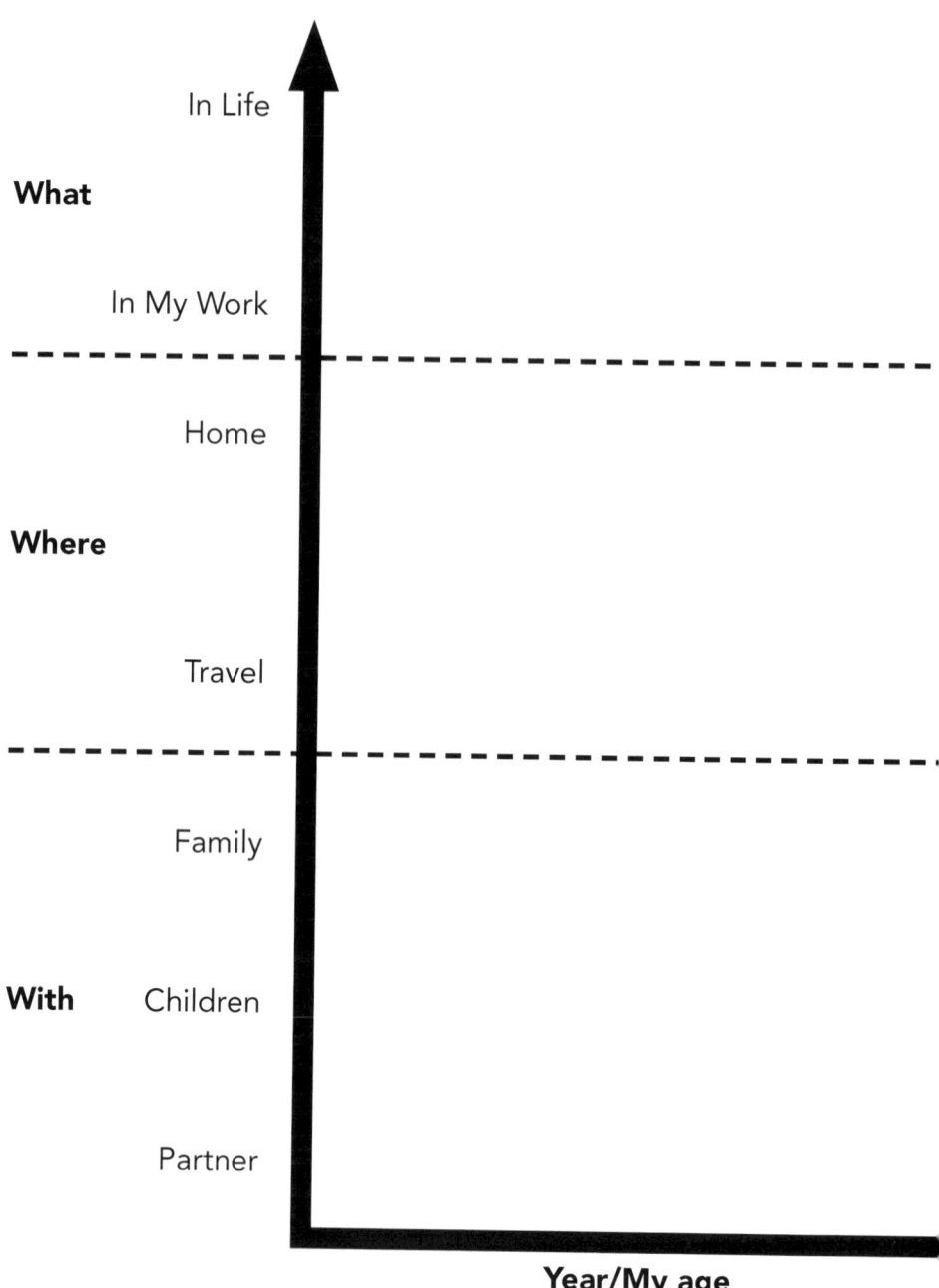

LIFE PLAN: MILESTONES

Draw your own 'bubbles' on the chart to capture the most important areas from your prioritisation grid.

Insert the key events and milestones

Life Plan: key milestone 2

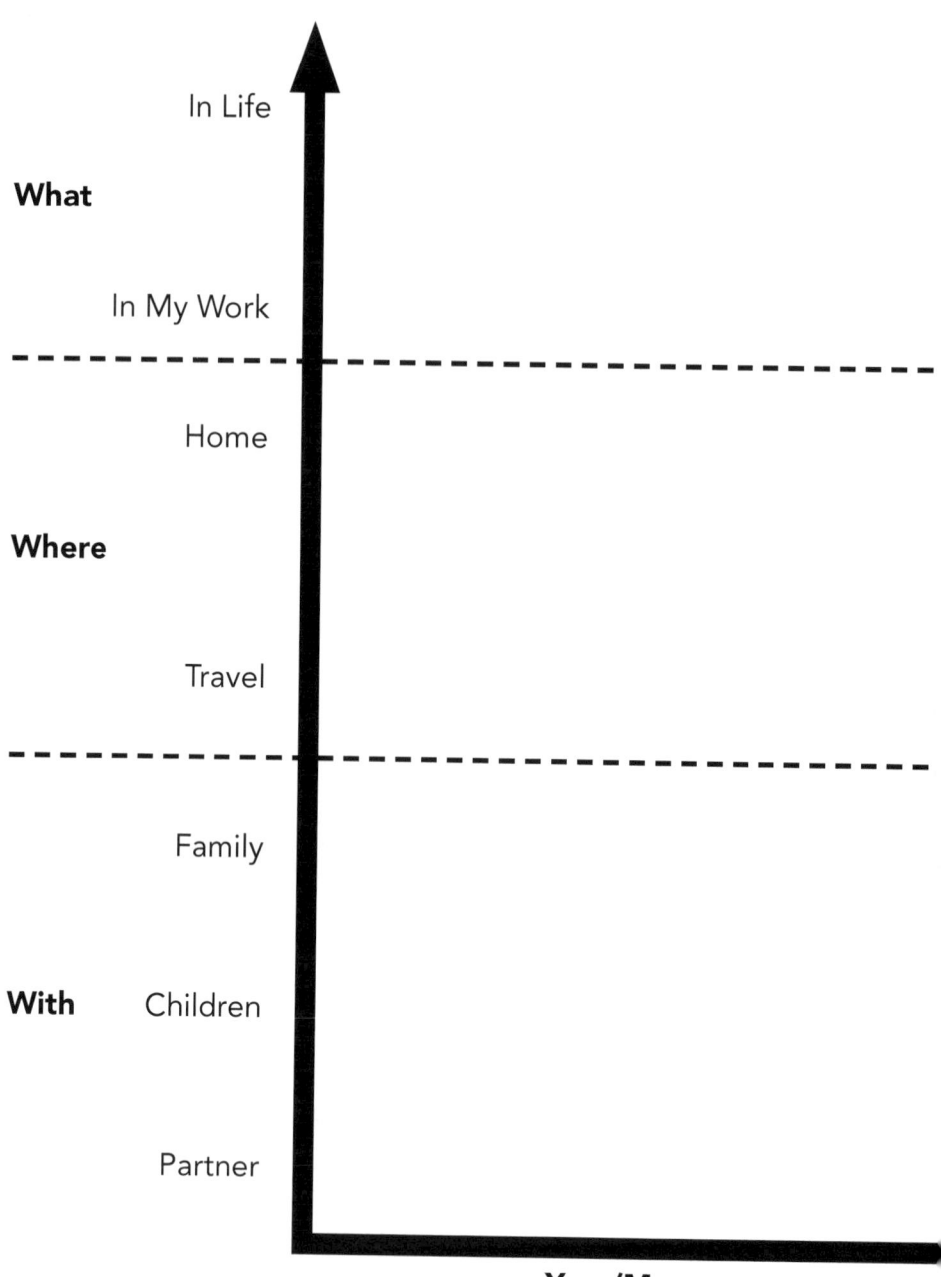

In Life

What

In My Work

Home

Where

Travel

Family

With   Children

Partner

Year/My age

Draw your own 'bubbles' on the chart to capture the most important areas from your prioritisation grid.

Insert the key events and milestones

WHEN

LIFE FINGERPRINT: WHEN

Pause now to reflect on your **When**, and complete the next part of your Life Fingerprint. What milestones have you set?

WHEN
What milestones have I set?

Next 12 months (list 5 key priorities)

1. _____
2. _____
3. _____
4. _____
5. _____

Milestone 1: _____
_____

(Top 5 priorities to achieve it)

1. _____
2. _____
3. _____
4. _____
5. _____

Milestone 2: _____
_____

(Top 5 priorities to achieve it)

1. _____
2. _____
3. _____
4. _____
5. _____

Sparks and Jolts

Chapter 8

Bringing it together in your Best Life Design

> 'Twenty years from now you will be more disappointed by the things you didn't do than by the ones you did do. So throw off the bowlines. Sail away from the safe harbour. Catch the trade winds in your sails. Explore. Dream. Discover.'
>
> **Mark Twain**

THE POWER OF BEING 100% YOU ...

As you will have seen throughout the book, I am a massive believer in strengths-based leadership and following your passions and dreams. When we have careers we enjoy, when we have hobbies and experiences we enjoy, and when we invest time with people we enjoy doing these things with, funnily enough we enjoy life more and start living our best life!

Best life planning is as simple as that. But the challenge is that most people's lives aren't like that. Many of us know our life is fine or okay, but it still feels like it's not as good as it could be – maybe it's 70% there but

30% needs work. Life Design is about life optimisation rather than life reinvention. If we focus on the areas that need a shift rather than trying to change everything we do, this makes Best Life Design more attainable.

We shouldn't confuse life optimisation with self-optimisation. Focusing on weaknesses, feeling judged or measured by others or feeling you could have done better is the unfortunate consequence of spending most of our lives dwelling on what we could improve on, instead of focusing on our strengths. It typically starts young with parental expectations, and continues into school, into university, into work and into retirement. This state of mind and state of being – of never being fully satisfied with who we are and what we uniquely bring to the world – brings with it feelings of being unfulfilled, worry, reduced confidence, status concerns and self-esteem issues, and ultimately, if not tackled, health issues.

At a simple level it can be a constant feeling of, *Is this as good as it gets?*, or, *I could have done more or been more.* Instead, we should focus on, *I am who I am so I better work out who that is, and I will shape and adapt my life to who I am rather than seeking to change myself to fit in.*

If you design your life for your unique Life Fingerprint there isn't another life anywhere that is the same match to what your optimal life looks like. Contrast that instead with being in chameleon mode seeking to shape yourself to other people's patterns; you will constantly be in a state of flux and living a suboptimal life.

> 'You only live once, but if you do it right, once is enough.'
> **Mae West**

FINALISING YOUR 6WS LIFE FINGERPRINT (WHO, WHAT, WITH, WHY, WHEN, WHERE)

Over the course of the book I've included tools and frameworks along the way to help you think through the component parts of your Best Life Design. Some of you will have paused as you read and completed the exercises, and many of you will have skimmed over them as you read on, planning to go back to them later. Either approach works … providing you do ultimately complete them and reflect on them.

Now is the time to go back and review again and complete each exercise. As you complete each exercise you can update your Life Fingerprints.

You can find the 10 exercises easily in the book because they are on the pages with the grey shading at the bottom. To recap, they are:

Chapter 2: Who

- My Life Line
- My Values
- My Strengths

Chapter 3: What

- My Sources of Inspiration
- My Life Wheel

Chapter 4: With

- My Energy Sources

Chapter 5: Why

- My Gifts and my Why

Chapter 7: When

- Autobiography and biography
- Life Plan 12 months
- Life Plan Milestones

Hopefully as you look at and reflect on your personal summary from the exercises, some patterns, 'a-ha' moments and Sparks and Jolts will start to emerge. I hope you are also starting to feel that being *you* and your Life Fingerprint is a great deal better and more positive than you ever gave yourself credit for!

LIVING YOUR E = MC²

So far in the book I've shared how Sir David Attenborough inspired me in Life Design. Let me add another great scientist to the list: Einstein. I had a realisation that the great Albert Einstein can not only teach us a lot about theoretical physics (after all, he is one of the smartest people who ever lived), I have rediscovered him in a new light, applying his quotes (and occasional mis-quotes) and words of wisdom to how we can find inspiration and live our best life. See if these words work for you too …

Be authentically you

'Strive not to be a success, but rather to be of value.'

'Most people say that is it is the intellect which makes a great scientist. They are wrong: it is character.'

'Great spirits have always encountered violent opposition from mediocre minds.'

Be curious and feed your imagination

'I have no special talent. I am only passionately curious.'

'The significant problems we face cannot be solved at the same level of thinking we were at when we created them.'

'Imagination is everything. It is the preview of life's coming attractions. Imagination is more important than knowledge.'

'Logic will get you from A to B. Imagination will take you everywhere.'

Stick with it and be open to learn from mistakes

'It's not that I'm so smart; it's just that I stay with problems longer.'

'In the middle of every difficulty lies opportunity.'

'A person who never made a mistake never tried anything new.'

'Information is not knowledge. The only source of knowledge is experience.'

Solve complex problems worth solving, but make sure the solution is simple

'If you can't explain it simply, you don't understand it well enough.'

'Any fool can make things bigger, more complex, and more violent. It takes a touch of genius – and a lot of courage – to move in the opposite direction.'

'If I had an hour to solve a problem and my life depended on the solution, I would spend the first 55 minutes determining the proper question to ask, for once I know the proper question, I could solve the problem in less than five minutes.'

'Everything should be made as simple as possible, but not simpler.'

'Insanity: doing the same thing over and over again and expecting different results.'

Live and enjoy the moment; be present

'There are only two ways to live your life. One is as though nothing is a miracle. The other is as though everything is a miracle.'

'I never think of the future – it comes soon enough.'

All those inspirational quotes got me thinking ... What if Einstein's great scientific breakthrough on the special theory of relativity ($E = MC^2$) could not just be used to explain the exponential energy release that created the atomic bomb, but to living our best life – would that work? So as per Einstein's words of wisdom, I 'stayed with my problem longer' and pondered upon how small changes create significant results, and I came up with this:

E is **Energy** – positive change in how I think, feel and act.

M is **Me** – I need to be open and receptive to new ideas and experiences.

C is **Collaboration** and **Continuous inspiration** from whatever and whomever inspires me.

2 is the **multiplier** of seeking out and feeling the effects of what inspires me. It's taking the time to really absorb inspiration in all its forms.

My final reflection from my pondering was, it's this final multiplier effect we don't always achieve and that we need to pay attention to. The need to pause, be present and take time for those things we find inspiring, whatever they are. What they are to each of us is highly personalised. We need to seek them out and appreciate them.

What are yours? Watching a TED Talk? Walking barefoot on the beach? Playing with the kids? Exploring something new?

Whatever they are, take time to work on your $E = MC^2$.

TOP FIVE ENABLERS OF BEST LIFE DESIGN

Whether you have read the book step by step doing each tool as you go, or have skim read the whole thing and will now re-read and do the exercises, there are five enablers I have found to be a key element of Life Design. The biggest is fear of change ... so we'll visit that one last.

Let's have a look at the top five enablers of Best Life Design.

1. Be curious, really curious

> 'We keep moving forward, opening new doors, and doing new things, because we're curious and curiosity keeps leading us down new paths.'
>
> **Walt Disney**

Look on situations in the past and in the now with intrigue and curiosity. Imagine yourself extracting yourself from a situation and looking in on it and analysing it. Our brain is not wired for curiosity; instead it creates short-cuts to deal with the 50,000 to 70,000 bits of stimulus we receive each day. Quick processing is needed rather than deep thought. Through thinking with curiosity, you can bypass using your reactive or amygdala part of the brain that jumps to an immediate conclusion and instead use your neocortex to think. Life planning takes curiosity, so that instead of using hardwired short-cuts we see instead new patterns emerge that we hadn't connected or joined the dots for previously.

2. Be kind to yourself as you start to reflect

> 'Be kind whenever possible. It is always possible.'
>
> **Dalai Lama**

My observation is that people, particularly girls and women, struggle to be kind to themselves. A good question to reflect on is, *would you treat others as harshly as you treat yourself?* Clues to this problem are in the language we use: 'I should' or 'I could' have 'seen this coming', 'I could have been a better mum … daughter … friend', 'I could have done better in my exams', and so on. If you are a perfectionist, be even kinder to yourself.

3. Be systematic: all 6Ws count!

> 'The mind is like an umbrella; it functions best when open.'
>
> **Walter Gropius**

If you haven't gone through and given each of the 6Ws time, revisit them. Why? Because they work together to define your Life Fingerprint, giving you a multi-dimensional plan to amplify *you*.

4. Start now, and I mean now …

> 'The start is what stops most people.'
>
> **Don Shula**

I find that some people get straight into Life Design, doing all the exercises and adapting and trying new ideas to hone their life plan. Others wait to start, waiting for some perfect condition to exist when they can do things: 'when I'm less busy', 'when the kids leave home', 'when I retire', 'when I have the money'. Procrastination kills progress, so get started! Start with something easy and practical, like a get together with one of your Energy Givers, or tackling your top priority on your Life Wheel. Progress is made one step at a time.

5. Using focus to beat fear

> 'Our greatest fear should not be of failure but of succeeding at things in life that don't really matter.'
>
> **Francis Chan**

So assuming you make the positive decision that you would like to make some changes and adjustments to your life, there is one final hurdle you need to overcome, and that is the fear of change that you will need to work through to be yourself or act on making a major change.

Why does fear kick in? Fear keeps us safe: if you are driving a car and someone stops in front of you, you slam on the brakes. No thought is required; your amygdala reaction kicks in. This is the same with pulling your hand away from something hot. But be aware our brain is triggered the same way for all change. Once we think about or consider something new our heart rate rises, and fear sets in. Our body senses all change as danger, so we need to move off automatic and hit the manual override switch.

The brain's response to fear is fight or flight. The fight or flight response is an acute stress response. It is our body's primitive, automatic, inborn response that prepares the body to 'fight' or 'flee' from perceived attack, harm or threat to our survival. Research has shown that fear of change activates our body's responses in the same way we react to danger. Even when our life is not in danger but our sense of fulfilment is, we tend to flee making a change because we are afraid of the 'danger' of change, sticking with the known versus the unknown.

One method to dealing with fear is to fight it with focus. In response to fear unfortunately fight and flight has a 10× multiplier over focus by way of response. Focus means focusing on the problem deeply and working it through step by step to get to a solution that works. If you spend a bit of time defining where the fear is coming from, and then tackle each area in turn, you can work on a practical plan to work it through.

At the core of it, when a person feels they want to change but they think it's impossible or too hard, the only way to do so is to identify the pattern of behaviour and then break it. How do you break a pattern? Identify it, decide it frustrates you, then get to the bottom of it, and then change it, and consciously make the decision, *I'm not going to let that get to me anymore*. Thinking through problems by deconstructing them in the neurolinguistic part of our brain means we can solve anything. Relying on our amygdala, which responds with fight and flight, will never let us push through to change.

> 'F–E–A–R has two meanings: "Forget Everything And Run"
> or "Face Everything And Rise." The choice is yours.'
>
> **Zig Ziglar**

The approach to facing fears can be learned … you can practise it. One proven method is to share your fears with others. Talk to your partner, talk to a friend, articulate your fears and then work on all the things you would need to do for the response to change from flight to facing it and making a change. To put fear in its place, try curiosity instead, and ask yourself *what if?* questions, or *how?* or *why not?* Being curious and assessing the risks and opportunities rationally puts fear back in its box.

Most of us know what we are not happy with, but defining it and being aware does not create change. Being able to be clear on what you'd rather it be creates a mindset shift. Once that's happened, it's possible.

I find common patterns in the range of options or solutions; you can immediately sense what's right for you because you know your 'Fingerprint'. For every fear or concern or frustration there is an opposing and opposite action that overcomes it: your decision and action to do something about it is what makes the difference.

THINK. PLAN. LIVE. THE JOURNEY AHEAD

Best Life planning is a constant work in progress. It is one of constantly thinking (both feeling and problem-solving kind of thinking) about what's working and what's not, planning what you want to shift and adjust, and then applying those adjustments to how you live. That is the essence of my *Think. Plan. Live.* philosophy. At the start of the book I shared my goal that by sharing approaches, exercises, frameworks and stories, my hope was that it would act as a stimulus or trigger in some small or big way so that you too would work out for yourself how you could design your best life.

> 'The best way to get something done is to begin.'
>
> **Anon**

My stories and journey so far represent my Life Fingerprint, and my future best life for my career has me focusing on seeking to help others work it out for themselves in regard to Life Design and leadership. My career is integrated alongside pursuing other life passions linked to family, nature, travel and art … My best life works for me.

My learnings so far from those people who have developed their best life through this approach is that once their life plan was created it has acted like a compass and navigator. The insights they learned about how to amplify themselves or recognise stressful situations that would be a trigger gave more clarity and less churn to both day-to-day and long-term choices in life. Further evolution will occur to build out your plan, but the core foundations do not change … because the patterns and behaviours manifested in your life were already well on the way to being shaped by the time you left school. So many of the clues to how we show up can be found in our past …

> 'Be the change that you wish to see in the world.'
>
> **Mahatma Gandhi**

My approach was initially targeted at people in their mid-forties to mid-fifties because that's a time not of a mid-life crisis but a mid-life reflection. Recently a number of coaching clients have asked me to take their sons and daughters through aspects of it too. What I have discovered is it works for them as well, particularly to navigate choices from a position of strength in knowing yourself. So my request to you is to think, *now I've completed the book, who else could it help?* And go help them do it too.

I hope the book helped you uncover, define and design your Best Life through your Life Fingerprint. Thanks for reading. Now it's time to put all that Thinking and Planning into Living …

Sparks and Jolts

Sparks and Jolts

Sparks and Jolts

Notes

Notes

More about Gill McLaren

Gill McLaren is on a mission to help people design and live their best life. Gill left a successful international corporate and a C-suite career because she felt she wasn't making enough difference to the world. She came to the realisation that through sharing her approach and coaching and running workshops with others to share her philosophies and method of Life Design, her practical approach really helped others create their own best life. It started with her team, then her colleagues and then her friends. The reaction was so positive to her approach to best life planning that she decided to set up a business and write a book to focus on it.

Respected as a successful and authentic leader in her business career, Gill rose to being one of fewer than 10 women out of over 100 in country general management roles globally at Coca-Cola. Gill also was a member of the Global Women's Leadership Council and Chair of the Pacific Women's Leadership Council, with a focus on the goal of achieving gender parity in senior leadership positions.

Her work and travel has taken her to all parts of the world: six continents and over 50 countries. During her career she has been based in the UK, Malaysia, Singapore and Australia. Her book draws on a deep cultural appreciation from her years living and working in diverse environments, and it also draws on her personal journey of navigating a successful career while being a devoted and passionate mum.

Gill is also a passionate speaker and opinion leader on the topics of Authentic Leadership, Women in Leadership and Shared Value Creation. Her speaking engagements have included television (Channel NewsAsia's *Perspectives* program) and radio ('Women of Worth' interview on 938Live Singapore).

On the topic of Shared Value and Public, Private partnerships she has spoken and facilitated at conferences including Sustainable Brands Kuala Lumpur, World Marketing Summit, CSR Asia Summit and the YSEALI Summit.

Gill engages her audiences with honesty, pragmatism, passion and humour. She's a big thinker and problem solver, and *Think. Plan. Live.* brings together learnings from her successful corporate career of 30 years with working in multicultural environments with a best life plan. The book is 'real', it covers ups and downs and twists and turns alongside tried and tested approaches to bring the reader something practical and fun.

Gill's approach is one that applies art and science and right and left brain thinking to life and career design, which she has translated into a strategic planning approach to Life Design in her 3-step Syntegrate model, which she shares with the readers in the book and in her consultancy, strategy and coaching business.

For more information please visit www.syntegrate.co.

The power of combining Coaching and Business Strategy

I believe there is great power at the intersection of Coaching and Personal development, Business Strategy and Consultancy.

Coaching and Development has always played a big role in my life. Throughout my corporate career the favourite part of my role as a leader was the development and growth of my team, because it is so rewarding to see others learn and grow. My role leading Women in Leadership as part of the Coca-Cola women's leadership council coaching translated also into advice and mentoring, and became deeper and more personal to my career journey and helping other women navigate their own life journey. But coaching and development on its own isn't enough. I find it can lack structure and purpose without really understanding each individual's personal goals and drivers of how they show up in the world.

Strategy in business has also been important to me, in a different way. Although I have spent time in varied business roles as well as in pure strategy roles, I have always been focused on how clarity of strategy guides and shapes thinking and results delivery. Through strategy I've always ensured I had a roadmap to reach my goals.

But strategy on its own isn't enough either. Being clear isn't enough without making sure the goal you're aiming for has enough personal purpose and meaning behind it. The strategy needs to excite you, and achieving it must make a difference.

Focusing on a blend of Strategy, Consultancy and Coaching makes complete sense to me, because I'm most inspired to explore ways of creating value at the intersection of Coaching and Development and Strategy, which is why I left the corporate world after nearly 30 years of business to set up Syntegrate.

Through Syntegrate I've developed a step-by-step approach adapted from strategic planning approaches I used in the business world and applied this to create my own unique coaching and personal consultancy approach. Strategy applied in business delivers results. Applied to coaching and personal development I find strategy enables people to define and achieve success in all aspects of their life. Helping people find clarity and purpose is much more rewarding to me than delivering a business plan … Making a positive, personal impact on everyone I coach lets them feel happier, and me feel happier too knowing that I made a difference.